THE KARDEA
Gourmet

SMART AND DELICIOUS
EATING FOR A
HEALTHY HEART

RICHARD COLLINS, M.D. AND ROBERT LEIGHTON
WITH SUSAN BUCKLEY, R.D.

Books are available for special promotions and premiums. For details,
contact Special Markets, LINX, Corp., Box 613, Great Falls, VA 22066,
or e-mail specialmarkets@linxcorp.com.

Book design by Paul Fitzgerald

Published by LINX

LINX, Corp.
Box 613
Great Falls, VA 22066
www.linxcorp.com

Printed in the United States of America

Nothing written in this book should be viewed as a substitute for
competent medical care. Also, you should not undertake any changes in
diet or exercise patterns without first consulting your physician, especially
if you are currently being treated for any risk factors related to heart disease
including high blood pressure, high cholesterol and diabetes.

Praise for
THE KARDEA GOURMET

"Highly recommended. Dr. Richard Collins is not only a
cooking cardiologist; he's a cardiologist's cardiologist. In this
lifesaving book, he shows that it's not just how long we live,
it's also how well we live."

> — **Dean Ornish, MD,** *Founder and President,
> Preventive Medicine Research Institute, Clinical
> Professor of Medicine, University of California*

"*The Kardea Gourmet* is predicated on sound principles
of nutrition, and high standards of cuisine - epitomizing
the opportunity I like to call 'loving food that loves us
back!' This book will help you get to that sweet spot - I
recommend it."

> — **David L. Katz, MD**, *Director, Yale University
> Prevention Research Center*

"If America followed the eating recommendations in *The
Kardea Gourmet*, we would not be talking about diabetes,
obesity, and heart disease like we are today. It's not just about
cutting back on the 'wrong' foods, but how to add heart-
healthy foods in doable ways. The Kardea Gourmet offers
science-backed dietary solutions, while at the same time
creating a more enjoyable eating experience."

> — **Glenn Gaesser, PhD,** *Director, Healthy Lifestyles
> Research Center, Arizona State University*

"*The Kardea Gourmet* is now my best prescription for healthy living and could easily be the difference between a premature heart attack and what the book could easily deliver - a long term relationship with your grandchildren!"

> — *James Ehrlich, MD,* *Clinical Associate Professor, University of Colorado*

"Diet plans that pay little attention to taste and satisfaction are difficult to live and typically fail. Not so with *The Kardea Gourmet.* This delightful book may be a game changer."

> — *Matthew M. Burg, PhD,* *Associate Clinical Professor of Medicine, Yale University School of Medicine, Columbia University Medical Center*

"*The Kardea Gourmet* provides a well-researched, simple yet elegant, no nonsense approach for improving your health for the rest of your life! "

> — *Jeffrey A. Morrison, MD, CNS*

"I'm always on the lookout for practical, evidenced based and easy to read sources of information and inspiration. I'll be recommending this book to just about all of my clients."

> — *Janice Baker, Registered Dietitian, Certified Diabetes Educator*

DEDICATION

*We dedicate this book to the researchers,
patient participants and others who continue
to advance our understanding of cardiovascular
health and heart disease prevention, and the
great chefs, farmers and food scientists who
make great tasting foods heart healthy.*

— Dr. Richard E. Collins, M.D.

*Dedicated to my wife and best friend,
Maureen Weaver, who has been a great supporter
of my passion to create Kardea; to my daughters,
Alexandra and Deanna, who are a never ending
source of joy and amazement, and to my parents
who reared my sister and me to celebrate family,
food and good health.*

— Rob Leighton

*Dedicated to my husband, Mark, whose love and
support nourishes me daily, and to my patients,
who continue to be my greatest teachers.*

— Susan Buckley, Registered Dietitian

CONTENTS

SECTION III: FROM TEXT TO TABLE - RECIPES

FOREWORD
ROB LEIGHTON, FOUNDER OF THE KARDEA GOURMET

Welcome to *The Kardea Gourmet* – a journey into a heart healthy lifestyle that finds its inspiration in a love of food, desire to keep things natural, belief in science, and passion for vital living.

The Kardea Gourmet starts its journey with two basic beliefs. Healthy eating is the foundation for long-term health and vital aging. Enjoying the foods we eat, each and every day, enriches our lives immeasurably.

The Kardea Gourmet is a collaboration of three people: a preventive cardiologist dedicated to keeping people healthy, a foodie and former chocolate executive with a cholesterol problem, and a registered dietitian who spends each day coaching people on heart healthy eating and weight loss.

Over a long career as a cardiologist, Mayo-clinic trained Dr. Richard Collins saw remarkable improvements in the profession's ability to save lives. Continuous advances in drugs and medical procedures allowed all cardiologists to improve their patients' odds for survival and recovery. Many of these same advances allowed doctors to identify individuals with developing heart disease and take action to prevent a heart attack or stroke.

Despite the great progress, a tragic trend has continued to accelerate. The number of Americans at high risk for heart attacks and strokes is growing. Central to this growing risk is the deteriorating eating patterns of Americans.

"I took a new view of my role," Dr Collins observed. "I no longer wanted to be a firefighter, saving lives as the blaze raged in the emergency room. I saw my new role as a forest ranger looking to prevent the fire and cultivate health."

Dr. Collins observed firsthand the power of Dr. Dean Ornish's integrated lifestyle approach to treating and reversing heart disease. Dr. Ornish's program integrates stress management, physical activity, and a disciplined plant-based, lowfat diet.

Dr. Collins brought the Ornish approach into his own practice. "The impact was impressive, but its success required a tremendous amount of restraint," recalls Dr. Collins. "Many people simply could or would not stay on this program for an extended period. While those at very high risk were motivated, for many others, the dietary disciplines proved too challenging."

Today Dr. Collins is the director of wellness at the unique South Denver Cardiology Associates in the Denver area. This 18 doctor practice offers an onsite membership fitness center and a gourmet breakfast and lunch bar. A wide atrium leads to broad multistory windows looking toward the Rocky Mountains and a meditation garden. It houses state-of-the-art technology, a spa, and a yoga center.

A truly exceptional aspect to Dr. Collins's practice is his role as "The Cooking Cardiologist." He conducts weekly cooking classes in the practice's full demonstration kitchen to help people adapt to and enjoy heart healthy eating.

His hands-on classes represent an unusual approach to Americans' deteriorating heart health. With people finding less time for home cooking and exercise and greater than ever cravings for heart harmful food, standard treatment options have increasingly relied on prescription medications and medical procedures.

As co-author with Dr. Collins, in 2005, when I turned 47, blood tests indicated my cholesterol levels bordered on high. This fact was hardly surprising. My mother's cholesterol was high enough for her to participate in a clinical trial for one of the leading cholesterol-lowering medications. Her mother had suffered multiple strokes, and her father died from a circulatory condition.

I was not philosophically opposed to taking medications. I believe that pharmaceuticals are one of the great achievements of the modern age. If I have an infection, I take antibiotics.

During summer months, I take an over-the-counter allergy pill. Cholesterol-lowering medication was different. It would need to be taken each and every day, possibly for the rest of my life.

It was more than just the length of therapy that bothered me. I wanted to avoid another, more disturbing medical trend. I watched my parents, both in their 80s, spend a significant portion of their day organizing the cocktail of medications prescribed by an array of physicians. Their primary care physicians deferred to specialists' recommendations, so no one assessed the quality of life for the whole person. They were merely a collection of separate but treatable ailments.

I was not ready to start down the road of daily drug treatment. I had concerns, not only about the side effects of or interactions among drugs but also that the pharmaceutical approach, delivered by a network of specialists, might create a downward spiral requiring even more medications. For example, my father's Parkinson's medication caused dizziness. This once active man who ran a marathon in his late fifties now couldn't exercise. His inactivity led to depression and loss of appetite. In turn this led to weight loss and anemia. The treatment? Prescription antidepressants and anemia medications.

I knew that if I wanted to avoid the same path, I had to actively engage in developing an alternative. As I considered various solutions, one of the great pleasures of my life played into my thoughts: my love for food. The kitchen is my artistic pallet.

For me, magic moments occur over a meal. Casual acquaintances turn into friends once they accept my invitation, "Can I cook for you?" Although I have little interest in shopping for clothes or gadgets, I will happily wander the aisles of gourmet food stores, farmers' markets, warehouse chains, and ethnic delicatessens. While my wife may curl up with a novel, I like to end the day with a good cookbook. Over the breakfast newspaper, I am as zealously outspoken about the published recipe as an article about world affairs.

This passion for good food is as much a part of my genetic

code as is high cholesterol. My father had always sought out foods for longevity, keeping canisters of raw nuts, seeds, and dried fruits next to the vitamins on the kitchen counter. The1970s Vitamin C revolution gave Linus Pauling the status of a star athlete in our home, and my mother spent years on a quest to find the perfect diet, sampling Stillman's high protein diet, Atkins' low carbohydrate diet, Weight Watchers and more. This environment informed the career choices of my sister and me. She is now a PhD epidemiologist with a focus on nutrition while I became president of one of the oldest continuously operating chocolate companies in the United States.

Combining the love of food and the desire to at least delay daily pharmaceuticals, I went in search of information on the role of nutrition in heart health. There is an abundance of data proclaiming the power of one diet or another to improve cholesterol levels and general heart health. Along with food products advertising their heart healthy quality, an extensive number of dietary supplements also claim to advance heart health. It took time to organize and distill the good information.

The Kardea Gourmet allows you to move more quickly along the learning curve. It explores the power of nutrition not simply in terms of cholesterol management, but also for blood pressure, inflammation, and blood sugar regulation. All of these factors play a role in long term heart and arterial health.

In fact, "Kardea" means *heart* in Greek. The traditional Mediterranean eating patterns are among the heart healthiest in the world. Food lovers like me applauded this discovery. It allowed previously forbidden pleasures – nuts, olives, olive oils, avocados, some amount of meat, even a daily glass of wine – to have a place on our plates. Heart healthy living could be delicious!

In the summer of 2009, Dr. Collins and I met to talk about our common passion for delicious, health promoting foods. We were dismayed by the conflicting and confusing information on nutrition and heart health.

What evolved from these discussions is *The Kardea Gourmet*, a guidebook on how foods and nutrients work to help – or harm – the health of the entire circulatory system.

The book delves into insights uncovered by researchers about Old World styles of eating. It covers the latest research in nutritional science, including plant-based diets, fiber, healthful fats and Omega-3s, antioxidants, and plant sterols.

Susan Buckley, a registered dietitian and nutrition educator who works with Dr. Collins, joined us to provide a unique perspective. Like myself, Susan speaks from personal experience. Over 15 years ago, she was 70 pounds overweight. Step-by-step, she shed those pounds in a year and has kept them off. Then a stay-at-home mom and part-time arts administrator, Susan's experience inspired her to resume her education and become a registered dietitian. Today, she integrates heart healthy nutrition and weight loss in changing patients' eating habits and attitudes. Along with understanding *what* they eat, she helps clients understand *why* they eat.

The recipes found in this book emphasize natural ingredients and whole foods, but they are only starting points. We also explore how different foods and nutrients are matched to create a heart healthy meal. Foods and flavors from around the globe provide new and exciting culinary options while you incorporate lifestyle improvements at your own pace. In addition, you can adapt food traditions from any culture to create a healthier diet for you and your family.

One last point: the Kardea approach is only one part of a toolkit in optimizing your health. It is not a replacement or excuse for other unhealthy habits. Use all the tools at your disposal – nutrition, exercise, weight management and when necessary, medications and medical interventions.

Human beings love to eat and eat well. *The Kardea Gourmet* will help steer your cravings for delicious foods to support long and vital living.

Foreword

DR. RICHARD COLLINS,
THE COOKING CARDIOLOGIST

I began my career as an interventional cardiologist fighting on the front lines of heart disease.

Practicing in Omaha, Nebraska, I routinely performed angioplasties. Through an artery in the leg, I would thread a catheter into the heart. The catheter had a balloon at the end which was then inflated, opening the artery. I might then insert a stent to hold the artery open. While these procedures continue to help many, other patients still required open heart surgery to bypass the diseased artery.

A turning point in my career came when I met a patient who had had his third bypass operation. He was in his sixties at this time and was looking for an alternative way of dealing with heart disease. Another operation was not an option. Such patients had limited prospects for years of vital living. This was back in 1993 when the concept of reversing heart disease was not widely accepted in the cardiovascular community.

In his search, this patient traveled to Sausalito, California to undergo an innovative treatment approach under Dr. Dean Ornish at the Preventative Medicine and Research Institute. The program had a number of components: a lowfat vegetarian diet, stress management and yoga, a support group, and exercise. All components were administered simultaneously. The results were astonishing. The patient lived until age 81 without any additional heart procedures.

That same year, I hung up my balloons and became a preventive cardiologist, establishing a preventive cardiology program in Omaha, Nebraska. The program was based on the multi-pronged approach of Dr. Ornish. We involved a regional medical center and gained support from the Mutual of Omaha insurance company.

Our experience was impressive and the results were published. The program saved the insurance company over $30,000 per patient (in 1995 dollars—health care costs have greatly escalated since then). Patients also avoided needless operations and procedures. Many of these patients also found themselves feeling better and healthier than they had in years. The program not only helped them move away from disease but also toward wellness and an improved quality of life.

It has been a long journey since 1993. Back then, the terms "yoga" and "lowfat vegetarian" were new to the cardiovascular community. Many refused to believe in the efficacy of the Ornish treatment, but a structured, multi-pronged lifestyle approach to heart disease has been steadily moving into the mainstream. In 2010, the Centers for Medicare and Medicaid Services (CMS) recommended the Ornish program for intensive rehabilitation therapy. After a sixteen-year review, the single largest insurance system in the United States now covers intensive lifestyle therapies. This coverage is only a first step, and the coverage will initially be only for the individuals with heart disease. I look forward to future steps that will extend coverage more broadly and take aim not simply at treatment, but also prevention.

My journey into preventive cardiology has taken me down unusual paths. As I worked with patients, I found that many had trouble maintaining the dietary requirements. While delivering proven benefits, the very lowfat, plant-based eating styles were too foreign and rigid to fit into their everyday lives. I began to help them discover, live, and love healthier eating, each day, each meal, and each snack. As a result, I became known as the Cooking Cardiologist, showing patients how to properly cook, eat well, control cholesterol, and have a very long and delicious life.

While healthy eating and cooking are the bedrock of my treatment, medications and interventional procedures are essential parts of an integrated and comprehensive approach to treating heart disease. Physical activity is crucial. Selected nutritional supplements have proven useful. Over the years, I have also seen the power of stress reduction and social support for improving the condition of heart patients. Through the continued works of Dean Ornish and many others, including Drs. Lance Gould, John McDougall, Neal Barnard, Herbert Benson, Caldwell Esselstyn Jr., and John Kabot Zinn, we have come to better understand the mind/body/heart and food connection. They too found the same results with the Dr. Ornish approach, all in separate research.

Along with an ever-expanding set of proven treatment options, there are increasingly better sets of tests and technologies to identify who is at risk for a heart attack or stroke, both in the short-term and over the coming decades. These assessment tools allow for improved treatment decisions adapted to the medical conditions and lifestyle choices of the patient.

And as a preventive cardiologist, I have learned one very important fact. Heart disease appears as we grow older, but it is not a disease of aging. It is a disease of living with factors that can damage our arteries — elevated cholesterol and blood pressure, excessive weight, inflammation and swings in blood sugars. The longer we live, the longer these factors have time to do their damage. Heart healthy eating is about addressing these factors throughout your life. Start young and keep working at it. *The Kardea Gourmet* will help you navigate the journey. Eat smart, eat delicious.

Chapter 1
THE HEART OF YOUR HEALTH: AN OVERVIEW

Mark Twain said, "The only way to keep your health is to eat what you don't want, drink what you don't like." Humorist Calvin Trillin took Twain's sentiments a bit further when he wrote "Health food makes me sick."

While both men are great wits, we believe that Twain and Trillin have it wrong. You can *crave* heart healthy eating!

Healthy eating is the foundation for a healthy heart.

Enjoying our foods is what allows us to maintain healthy eating from day-to-day and meal-to-meal.

Does this sound like a pipe dream? It doesn't have to be. *The Kardea Gourmet* will show you how mostly healthy ingredients create healthier, delicious recipes. We will show you how to use these healthier recipes to make even healthier meals.

Many of us enjoy foods that delight the senses but are harmful. We consume these foods in their processed and prepared forms. We devour them in fast food restaurants and even feast on them in the most trendy bistros. We eat them as salted natural snacks, highly sweetened granolas, and organic cheeses. We eat these foods for the joy they provide and as part of a celebration of life.

Defining Heart Healthy Eating

What is heart healthy eating? Experts agree that heart healthy eating starts with a plant-based foundation.

You may have heard about the Mediterranean diet as being heart healthy. Many believe this diet is about the generous use of olive oil. It involves far more than that: while the diet includes some olive oil, lean meats, cheese and other dairy, fish and eggs, true heart healthy Mediterranean eating is plant-based, with vegetables, fruits, and grains playing a much larger role than in the standard American diet.

The blood pressure lowering DASH (Dietary Approaches to Stop Hypertension) or the cholesterol lowering National Cholesterol Education Program (NCEP) diets sponsored by the National Institutes of Health (NIH) and endorsed by the American Heart Association (AHA) build on a plant-based foundation, but also allow you to eat most anything within moderation, provided you also enjoy mostly fruits, vegetables, and whole grains. The NIH reports that health benefits of these diets can be comparable to the results from medications.

There are also purer plant-based diets, variations of which are presented by leading physicians and academic researchers, such as Dean Ornish, MD; T. Colin Campbell, PhD; Joel Fuhrman, MD; Caldwell Esselstyn, MD; John McDougall, MD; and others. These diets are therapeutic and are used to treat people with serious heart conditions. Allowing little if any animal-based products and very limited amounts of fats -- even "good" fats -- has even been found to reverse heart disease. These purer plant-based diets also drive down cholesterol and blood pressure levels, help address diabetes and metabolic syndrome, and can lead to substantial weight reduction.

There has been much argument over the right balance of the macronutrients in the United States. Unlike micronutrients, such as vitamins and minerals which the body requires in smaller amounts, we use large quantities of macronutrients consisting of proteins, carbohydrates, and fats for calories and energy. Should you be on a lowfat diet? A high protein diet? A low carbohydrate diet? These are simply the wrong questions, leading to diet "solutions" that have caused real harm for many Americans.

The right question is: How can you build eating patterns upon a plant-based foundation? This question is not about being vegetarian. Even a vegetarian can have unhealthy, fattening eating patterns. It is about utilizing vegetables, fruits and whole grains, foods that overall are lower in calories and higher in fiber, vitamins, minerals, and the untold number of nourishing compounds that support a healthy heart. Building on this dietary foundation, the question of the appropriate amount of foods that can bring great delight to eating -- meats, cheese, sugars, salt -- will vary and should be explored based on individual risks.

No single path to the heart healthy, plant-based foundation exists, and no one "diet" is appropriate for everyone. Different people will start their journey to plant-based eating from different places.

Tastes certainly vary. Those loving meat and potatoes or macaroni and cheese start from a different place than those craving oatmeal and salads. Daily pressures in the context of hectic lifestyles help define whether you choose fast food on the run or a wholesome, home-cooked meal. Budgetary realities are other very real factors. In America, eating healthy is simply more expensive.

Risks for heart disease and stroke also vary. Some people find themselves at low risk, others at intermediate risk, and still others face the imminent prospect of a heart attack or stroke. The factors contributing to these risks also differ – cholesterol, blood pressure, blood sugar regulation, weight, and levels of inflammation fluctuate from one person to another.

Depending on your body chemistry, different nutrients can cause significantly diverse changes in these factors. Sodium found in salt can result in major escalation in blood pressure for some and a much more modest increase in others. Simple carbohydrates that can cause rapid rises in blood sugars can be well-regulated in some, but can cause unhealthy swings in others, creating serious issues for the entire circulatory system. Certain "bad fats" bring about a sharper increase in cholesterol in some; in others, "good fats" like the Omega-3s in fish and monounsaturated fats found in olive and canola oil, can more favorably affect cholesterol levels and healthy functioning in the arteries.

Building Towards a Plant-Based Foundation

So how should you begin your journey to satisfying heart healthy eating? A good place to start is with this book: *The Kardea Gourmet* provides information and insights that will allow you to more consciously define your own heart healthy pattern of eating.

We'll start with an understanding of the healthiest diets -- those that Twain and Trillin would probably distain. These are the lowfat, plant-based diets. All meat, dairy products and vegetable oils -- even olive oil -- are restricted. Higher fat, plant foods such as nuts, seeds, olives, and avocados are only used in moderation, if at all. Overall, these diets can maximize the intake of the nutrients that help, minimize the intake of nutrients that harm, and deliver foods that gram-for-gram are substantially lower in calories. With a strict discipline around these diets, you can eat substantial quantities and maintain a healthy weight. Moreover, you are likely to see dramatic improvements in cholesterol, blood pressure, blood sugar, and inflammatory levels. Even people who assumed that they are genetically destined to live with high cholesterol or high blood pressure can see tremendous improvements, in many cases to levels where they can avoid the use of medications.

The journey from healthiest to harmful can be a winding road. The path begins with a gentle slope downward. At some point, though, a rising amount of calorie-dense, heart damaging foods and the falling levels of foods with beneficial nutrients cause a sharp decline in healthy eating patterns. The body becomes overwhelmed as a heart harmful diet drives up weight, blood pressure, cholesterol, and causes blood sugar levels to swing widely.

Researchers like T. Colin Campbell highlighted the power of lowfat, plant-based diets in studies of traditional populations.[1]

Pioneering doctors such as Dean Ornish, Caldwell B. Esselstyn Jr., and Joel Fuhrman have shown how these diets not only dramatically reduce heart risk factors -- high cholesterol and blood pressure, inflammation, excessive weight, and poorly controlled blood sugar -- but also can reverse heart disease and other chronic diseases such as Type 2 diabetes.[2, 3, 4] In his own practice, Dr. Richard Collins has shown that in addition to reversing heart disease, these dietary approaches can have a greater impact on outcomes than even inserting a stent or angioplasty.

After an extensive and extended review, the Centers for Medicare and Medicaid Services (CMS) recently concluded that the Ornish and Pritikin lifestyle programs meet the standard for an "intensive cardiac rehabilitation" program and should be eligible for reimbursement.[5] America's leading health insurer now affirms the dramatic effectiveness of these structured dietary approaches.

Using purer plant-based diets as the heart health optimizing standard, The Kardea Gourmet moves toward more enjoyable eating. Step-by-step, we ease up on certain restrictions, expanding the opportunities for sensory delight, as illustrated in Figure 1.1.

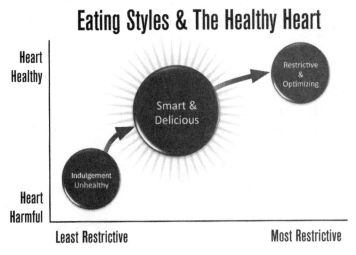

Figure 1.1. Eating Styles and the Healthy Heart

You can achieve both a healthy and delicious diet through smart eating.

Research on the traditional diets of the eastern Mediterranean, southern Japan, rural China, and Greenland reveal a very low incidence of heart disease. All are based on less processed, more natural foods with lower levels of salt and saturated and trans fats than found in the standard American diet. With the exception of eating patterns in Greenland, which are very high in heart healthy Omega-3 fatty acids, complex and fiber-rich carbohydrates found in vegetables or grains serve as the dietary foundation. All diets included some meats, fish, simple sugars, and salt.

But there are sharp differences. Some countries have minimal levels of total fat, while others include high levels. Some are low in all proteins, while still others eat only small amounts of animal proteins.

The dissimilarities are mostly due to the variation of available food within each culture. The people of the Mediterranean enjoy red wine, nuts, and olive oil. The native peoples of Greenland traditionally savored large amounts of fish and seal oil. The Okinawans of Southern Japan relished yams, soy, and green tea. These favorite foods bring different nutrients to heart healthy diets. In understanding these differences, Kardea finds the flexibility to create great tasting foods. Unfortunately as these populations have adopted modern diets, they have seen an increase in heart disease and strokes.

The National Institutes of Health (NIH) recognize the power of a mixed but properly balanced diet to promote heart health. Through the National Cholesterol Education Program (NCEP) the NIH has issued dietary recommendations for preventing and treating heart disease, stating that nutritional approaches to cholesterol management can be "comparable to many cholesterol medications."[6] The NIH also reports that healthier eating can achieve blood pressure reductions similar to drug therapies.[7] Eating patterns can play a central role in the progress or prevention of diabetes, metabolic syndrome, and plaque promoting inflammation in the arteries.

Eating for *Your* Heart Health

You can significantly reduce your odds of heart disease -- regardless of your family history -- by journeying towards a plant-based eating foundation.

You may have already tried to make this shift to some degree. You are eating less red meat. You've switched to skim dairy products to avoid saturated fats. You've acquired a taste for tofu, lots of fresh vegetables, and a range of whole grains. You looked into the Mediterranean diet and learned that some fats, like olive oil, are better for your heart health. You now satisfy your yen for bread and butter with a crusty baguette dipped, but not doused, in olive oil. You may also enjoy other heart healthy foods, such as oat cereals in the morning and a salmon entrée in restaurants.

Additionally you might be consuming specific nutrients like Omega-3s, plant sterols, antioxidants, potassium, and soluble fibers in the form of supplements or fortified foods.

The good news is that your efforts have probably improved your heart health.

But if you are like many Americans, your diet is still far from heart healthy. Your family's eating patterns may not be as damaging as they once were, but may still not be protecting your heart health. Today most Americans eat too many harmful and not enough helpful nutrients and too many calorie-rich foods. Today, death and disability from heart disease remains stubbornly higher than levels found in the societies that once enjoyed a heart healthy style of eating.

While Americans recognize the need to eat healthy, and in fact 81 percent feel that they are well informed about ways to support heart health, fewer than half chose heart healthy foods when dining out or shopping for groceries.[8] Only 37 percent stock their kitchens with heart healthy foods.

Today a large and growing percentage of Americans are at significant risk for heart disease. Only 7.5 percent of Americans find themselves at low risk for heart disease, which is down from 10.5 percent from the late 1980s.[9] Many who had been at low risk have moved to moderate risk. Others at moderate risk have moved to high. Only through remarkable gains in medical technology have we been able to avoid an upswing in the death and disabilities associated with heart disease. A consistent flow of new drugs and medical techniques allow doctors to address rising risks. As a nation, we increasingly look to medicine to save us from ourselves at increasingly high and potentially non-sustainable costs.

How Did We Get Here?

We have come to this point for many reasons. Perhaps the most significant cause lies in the American love of consuming. The traditional heart healthy diets of the Mediterranean and Asia evolved in very localized societies. They ate what was available, not what they craved. Today we have far greater choices from all over the world.

But such an array has a downside. There is great availability of heart harmful foods not found in more traditional societies. Along with lacking the helpful nutrients, a few small bites deliver artery damaging bad fats and bad carbohydrates, salt, and a substantial number of calories.

Cost also drives our choices. Mass-produced and highly processed foods can be far cheaper than nutrient-rich, natural alternatives. Consider how many fast food chains deliver prepared and packaged meals for only a couple of dollars while a similar-sized serving of uncooked vegetables costs more in a grocery store. No wonder nutritionally related diseases in America have a class component. Along with being obese and overweight, the poor and struggling middle class have a higher incidence of high blood pressure and Type 2 diabetes than those with higher incomes.

And because of their hectic, on-the-go lifestyles, fewer Americans prepare their own meals. The shopping, cooking, and cleaning involved is simply another household chore that can be avoided through bringing in food and eating out as well as purchasing prepared and frozen meals at the grocery.

Thirty years ago, meals took more than an hour to prepare; now the time is cut in half to an average of 30 minutes. Over 90 percent of Americans own a microwave oven — great for heating highly salted, pre-processed meals. Interestingly, thirty years ago, men in the kitchen took 15 minutes to prepare a meal, and take exactly the same amount of time now. While more men may have rightly found their way into the kitchen, their presence may not have helped our nutritional health.

While Americans love consuming, they have become less engaged with the actual enjoyment of eating. Watch people in a restaurant. Time and again they are "multi-tasking," reading a book, talking, texting, or looking out into space. The only time many people really pay attention to their food is when they put it into their mouths. Even more striking is the 1,200 calorie fast-food breakfast. But for the greasy aftertaste and the empty containers, many have no memory of the meal. They simply devour it, focus on the road and the day's challenges, the radio, and the incoming cell call.

In traditional societies, the hard work of securing and preparing foods demanded a daily celebration. Eating was a focus for social activity and, rather than being a casual event, was cherished and appreciated.

Diverse Paths to a Healthy Heart

Each of us has different tastes, risks, and lifestyle preferences. So how do you find your own path to heart healthy, plant-based foundation?

Start by asking the right questions. Whether you should be following a lowfat or a low carbohydrate or a high protein *diet* is categorically the *wrong* question and may result in heart harmful eating. Asking about the *quickest* way to lose weight can be just as counterproductive.

So what *are* the right questions? You are looking to discover which issues first need to be addressed to most effectively advance your health, today and over time.

- How does food and nutrition help or harm my heart and arteries? How can nutrition affect key risk factors -- cholesterol, blood pressure, diabetes and metabolic syndrome, and inflammation?
- What are my risks? Do I have a family history of heart disease? Do I already have heart disease? Do I have high blood pressure, diabetes, or high cholesterol?

By answering these questions, you begin your journey and start focusing on changing your eating habits and patterns (see Figure 1.2). It is has taken years to define your preferences and establish cravings for specific foods so it will take time to reprogram your tastes. With your knowledge of the power of nutrition and an understanding of your personal risks, you can continue this journey. And in time, you should find yourself preferring the better-for-you foods.

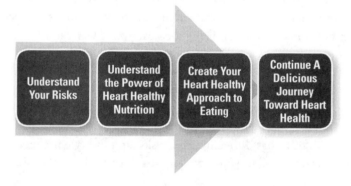

Figure 1.2. Smart and Delicious Eating for a Healthy Heart – The Journey Begins

If you are highly motivated to optimize your heart and circulatory health, you might want to adopt a more restricted plant-based diet. If you already have been diagnosed with heart disease, this approach to eating provides effective treatment.

However, many of us want greater freedom in partaking in all sorts of foods. We want to enjoy nuts, seeds, avocados, and olives. Healthier vegetable oils such as extra virgin olive oil also can dramatically enhance the taste of recipes. While high in calories, these foods are still rich in heart helpful nutrients.

Some meat, fish and shellfish, eggs, dairy, and some sugars and sweet syrups can also be added to healthy, delicious eating. But with the increased calorie density in these foods, you'll need to control how much you eat. These foods also introduce heart harmful compounds while delivering lower levels of the heart helpful nutrients. Yet they remarkably expand culinary options and substantially increase enjoyment. Even Mark Twain might have gotten pleasure from this type of eating.

Is this still a heart healthy diet? Actually, it embodies the definition of the Mediterranean diet. It still meets heart healthy standards defined by the National Institutes of Health and the American Heart Association. For individuals maintaining this style of eating for many years, research has shown substantially lower risk for heart disease. These diets also dramatically reduce risks of heart attacks and strokes even for those with known heart disease.

The challenge is that the gates are now open. Under the restricted plant-based diet, the standards of what should be eaten are clear. Eat only fruits, vegetables, beans and grains, and perhaps some nuts and seeds.

Under the mixed diet, however, the standards are less defined. You now need to think about avoiding simple carbohydrates that cause a rush of sugar into the bloodstream. You'll also have to consider limiting the calorie-rich fats that can increase cholesterol and contribute to weight gain as well as become more conscious of the risks of excessive salt intake. You also must take into account whether you are getting a sufficient amount helpful nutrients.

With regard to the latter, you may have heard that you should be eating a certain number of servings of fruits, vegetables, and whole grains each day. But what is the right portion size for a serving? How many servings did you eat today? Or yesterday? Was it the right amount? One-half of the desired amount? One quarter?

Between these many decisions and your hectic lifestyle, you may lose your nutritional balance, elevating your risks for heart disease. The level of calorie-rich, heart harmful foods now dominate. The levels of helpful foods delivering the necessary nutrients may have fallen by the wayside.

The Kardea Gourmet will help you eat "smart and delicious" for a healthy heart. *The Kardea Gourmet* is not a "program." Unlike so many diets, it is not something that you start, lose some pounds, and then stop. Rather, it is a philosophy of eating that keeps deliciousness, risks, and science in balance as you journey toward heart healthy eating.

Every Meal Counts!

Beyond *what* we eat, there is tremendous power in *how* we eat. Eating itself triggers a wide range of complex reactions in the body. These are essential for life but the body has developed sophisticated systems to keep these reactions in control. Helpful nutrients serve to support these control mechanisms. Harmful nutrients and excessive calories can work to overwhelm them, leading to risk of arterial damage.

In modern America, unhealthy ingredients are combined into less healthy recipes to create even unhealthier meals. Part of the power of the heart healthy diets found in traditional societies lies with the fact that all meals -- breakfast, lunch, dinner, and even snacks -- blend sufficient amounts of healthy nutrients to minimize the impact of the harmful foods. Smart and delicious eating builds on this understanding.

If you're looking to break away from heart harmful eating, *The Kardea Gourmet* will blend an understanding of the power of nutrition with the view that "purely healthy" eating may be an unrealistic goal. This book recognizes the love of eating and eating well.

The Kardea Gourmet will teach you how to match delicious foods that are good for you with those you love (but may not love you back). It will help foster a more controlled burn rather than igniting a wild blaze. It will provide you with a keener grasp of how foods come together to help or harm and will help you better identify the dietary changes needed for your body chemistry and risk profile.

The Role of Supplements

We focus on building heart healthy *eating* into your lifestyle, but supplements also can play a useful role. Some make even the most therapeutic diets more powerful in advancing heart health while others complement the medications prescribed by your doctor. Medical science has established that selected nutrients -- Omega-3s, certain types of fiber, plant sterols, potassium, and antioxidants -- can play a critical role in advancing heart health.

However, supplements are just that; rather than being a replacement or solution, they add to the effectiveness of changes in eating patterns and other forms of treatment. Supplements cannot overcome the adverse impact of an overly indulgent, unhealthy diet. Rather they provide some fortification to a smart and delicious diet, bringing it closer to becoming optimizing and therapeutic.

With the help of your doctor, it is up to you to define what to put into your body. As illustrated in Figure 1.3, foods, dietary supplements, and medications all represent powerful chemicals. Over the years, the repeated use of any of these compounds may have a significant effect -- good or bad -- on health and wellness. The more risk factors you have, the more aggressive you should be in reducing your chances of a heart attack or stroke. Some will choose a step-by-step approach. Others will look to make more dramatic changes. You and your doctor will need to determine the pace of change.

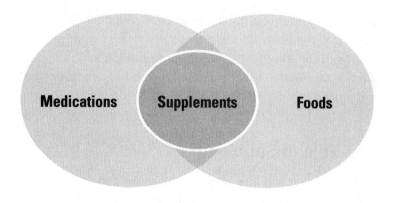

Figure 1.3. Integrating Foods, Supplements, and Medications

Those adopting a disciplined plant-based diet for heart health will experience significant weight loss without counting calories. For those looking to remain within the smart and delicious range, quantity still counts. You will need to be mindful of calorie counting or portion control. Similarly, you should avoid mindless eating -- when your food is consumed without thought or conscious enjoyment.

You will need to become a mindful eater, eating when you are hungry, but not beyond the point of contentment. Eating until you are full is eating too much. The feeling of being "full" is your body's way of telling you that you have overindulged.

Using and Cooking with *The Kardea Gourmet*

The Kardea Gourmet is organized into three sections. The first section provides an understanding of heart attack risks. One in three Americans will die from a heart disease or stroke. Countless others will have the quality of their lives compromised. What is the likelihood that you will be one of these statistics?

We start by exploring some basic biology, then delving into the way various risk factors – high cholesterol, high blood pressure, inflammation of the arteries, and swings in blood sugar – can work together to damage heart health. We then translate this general understanding of risk into insight for *your* individual risks for heart disease, a heart attack, or a stroke — in the near term or in the future. How your doctor determines whether you are at low, intermediate, or high risk is also covered.

Section II discusses how eating impacts your risk factors. The power of individual nutrients to help or harm, the workings of good and bad fats and carbohydrates as well as sodium and potassium, and appropriate levels of protein, along with the roles of Omega-3s, antioxidants, plant sterols, fiber, and other heart healthy nutrients are described. The second section closes with some insights into weight management. Excessive weight causes multiple complications related to heart health and may be the most pressing issue associated with your health and well-being. However, rather than focusing narrowly on weight loss, work towards establishing healthy eating habits. Weight loss and control are part of the larger framework.

In Section III, The Kardea Gourmet moves from text to the table, helping you rethink your eating patterns and choices. "Matching foods" for improving the nutritional balance; dramatic versus incremental changes in eating behaviors; snacking for heart health rather than heart harm; how beverages can be a powerful agent of heart health; foods in their various forms -- natural vs. organic, raw vs. cooked, fresh vs. stored; and how to incorporate so-called forbidden foods into your diet can be found here. Also included are delicious recipes to create even healthier meals. We take you on a tour of the Mediterranean – from Spain and France to Greece, Lebanon and Israel and then on to Morocco. We show you how to make the great meals from these regions even healthier.

How long will it take to obtain measurable improvements? It is up to you. You can see results with a few simple changes in a few weeks. Blood pressure reductions can come quickly; sometimes within two weeks of engaging in heart healthy eating.[10] Meaningful cholesterol reductions or improvements in blood sugar control may take a bit longer, perhaps four weeks. Most importantly, you will need to stay the course. Heart healthy eating should span a lifetime; the exact opposite of a crash diet.

So prepare to embark upon a great tasting journey that can add delight and joy to your life. It also is a serious one that requires monitoring and checking with routine testing and tracking.

The Kardea Gourmet is about helping you adapt your lifestyle over time. It has taken years to develop your current eating habits and cravings and add those extra pounds. It will take time to rewire your cravings and habits. This book allows you to navigate the steady course--even when life's pressures may force an occasional detour.

The first steps on the road to heart healthy eating involve identifying those adjustments to your eating habits that are both easy to maintain on a daily basis along with those that are most important to your particular condition. As these changes become habits, you can move toward a cardiovascular health optimizing style of eating and alter your cravings, the hardwiring of eating patterns from childhood.

This book will help you push beyond smart and delicious eating to heart optimizing and therapeutic eating. Perhaps not every day and perhaps not at every meal, but you can learn how good-for-you foods can be something that you prefer, even crave.

SECTION I:

UNDERSTANDING YOUR RISKS

| Understand Your Risks | Understand the Power of Heart Healthy Nutrition | Create Your Heart Healthy Approach to Eating | Continue A Delicious Journey Toward Heart Health |

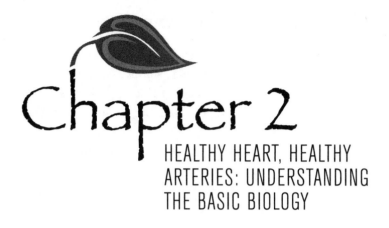

Chapter 2

HEALTHY HEART, HEALTHY ARTERIES: UNDERSTANDING THE BASIC BIOLOGY

The cardiovascular system is amazing and complex, supporting all activity in the body. It delivers oxygen and nutrients, removing carbon dioxide and toxins. The blood flow speeds up during exercise and slows down when at rest. It also is one of the primary pathways through which the immune system delivers its agents to all parts of the body.

Cardiovascular events, like heart attacks and stroke, remain the leading cause of death and disability in the United States. Cardiovascular health also is a keystone to healthy aging and long-term vitality. Other chronic diseases like dementia and kidney disease are linked to a diminished cardiovascular system.

Genetics play a role in the overall health of the heart and arteries. Some people smoke, gain weight, and eat poorly, but they have "good" genes. They live long, active lives without suffering from heart disease. Others may lead a highly disciplined lifestyle designed to promote heart health. Yet they may still suffer cardiovascular disease, perhaps early in life.

For most of us, however, our hearts' future is foretold by more than genetics. The interplay between individual body chemistry and lifestyle choices define whether the heart and arteries remain healthy. The level of exercise, weight, type of food, medications, and dietary supplements can turn on, turn off, slow down, or speed up the process.

Challenged Arteries, Threatened Heart

Blood flows from the heart through the arteries and returns through the veins. Arteries however, are more than simple pathways. An artery is a complex organ consisting of three layers -- the primarily protective outer layer, the middle layer of muscle which does much of the work, and the third, inner layer, the endothelium. Once thought to be only a thin layer of inactive cells providing a non-stick surface to help the blood flow easily, the healthy endothelium, in fact, plays a major role in the functioning of the arteries.

When the heart is beating faster because of stress or exercise, the arteries will dilate, or open wider. This allows the blood to flow more freely. The arteries constrict during more relaxed periods, easing the amount of work the heart muscle must do to get oxygen and nutrients to the body. A healthy endothelium plays a major role in regulating this process. The endothelium also plays a role in controlling the "stickiness" of the blood and whether a harmful blood clot might form in an artery.

Generally, everyone is born with clear and healthy arteries. Years of living take their toll. A complex set of processes starting early in life challenge arterial health. Slowly in some people, faster in others, these processes lead to the creation of plaque that can narrow the arteries, as illustrated in Figure 2.1. As we live longer, this process has more time to do damage.

Increasing Risks of Life-Threatening Plaque

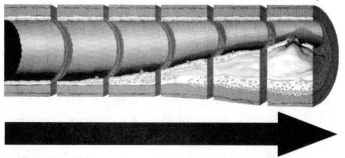

**Plaque Starts to
Develop in First
Decade of Life**

**Extensive Plaque
Developement by
Fourth Decade**

Figure 2.1: Timeline for Plaque Development (Adapted from C Pepine, *American Journal of Cardiology*, 1998; 82 Suppl 10A)

As we age, narrowed arteries may no longer meet the demands for blood oxygen during exercise or stress. When this happens to arteries within the heart, chest pain known as angina occurs.

Sometimes plaque builds to the point of fully closing the artery in the heart. If this occurs in one of the smaller arteries, it can lead to a weakened heart. Even at rest, the heart cannot pump enough blood to the body. This condition is known as congestive heart failure. People can live for many years with this condition, but the quality of life can be sharply compromised.

If a blockage occurs in a major artery, you may face a life-threatening heart attack. In your brain, the same process can cause a stroke.

Where a healthy endothelium was once able to support the healthy functioning of the arteries, plaque now exists. In time, this plaque surface hardens, or calcifies, causing the arteries to be less flexible. They are now less able to dilate and constrict, placing stress on the heart.

The medical community is intensely focused on identifying and then clearing arteries with extensive plaque. Resting electrocardiograms, stress tests, angiograms, and heart scans all work towards uncovering these conditions, while bypass surgery and angioplasty help remedy them. These tests and procedures have saved countless lives and prevented an untold number of heart attacks and strokes.

But the frustrating truth is that many heart attacks and strokes occur in individuals who do not have extensive narrowing of the arteries! In fact, 50 percent of heart attacks occur when arteries are less than 50 percent narrowed. Each day, many Americans are tested for heart disease and the extensive buildup of plaque and neither are identified. It takes a 75 percent narrowing of the artery before someone will fail a stress test. The harsh fact is that many people will pass routine heart tests and believe they are not at risk of a heart attack. Only when they are stricken within months, weeks, or even days of these tests, do they recognize that heart attack prevention requires greater vigilance to health and wellness.

Interestingly, others have considerable buildup of plaque, even to the point where the arteries in their heart are significantly narrowed. They live long lives without suffering a heart attack.

Stable versus Unstable Plaque

Contrary to popular belief, rather than being the result of gradual plaque buildup, many heart attacks occur when the plaque "ruptures." Unstable plaque is like a pimple on the skin. It can rupture or explode at any time. Following a rupture, clots develop. Sometimes only a small clot will be created. It does not significantly hinder the blood flow. Like any wound, the rupture will heal itself.

Other times, the clot completely blocks the flow of blood. This can happen near where the rupture occurred. Clots also can break free and get lodged elsewhere. When a clot lodges in an artery, the area of the body depending on its blood flow is then damaged or dies. This can happen almost anywhere in the body -- the heart, the brain, the lungs, even in the arms and legs.

No doubt, the risks are greater when the artery is already narrowed by the buildup of plaque. A smaller clot can cause a complete blockage in a narrowed artery. Frequently though, the level of plaque buildup can still be quite low, perhaps only 20 percent. Yet, the clot is sufficiently large to completely block the flow of blood.

Increasingly, plaque is understood as stable or unstable. Stable plaque quietly lines the arteries. Like a scar tissue, it is a sign of past damage, but it may not pose a threat. Unstable plaque is more like an infection of the skin. Left untreated, it will likely cause a problem.

Medical testing, however, is best at identifying the existence of significant amounts of plaque. It does not yet do as good a job in distinguishing between unstable and stable plaque. And it often does not identify low levels of unstable, life-threatening plaque.

What we do know is that four factors -- cholesterol, elevated blood pressure, high and widely fluctuating blood sugar levels, and inflammation -- are key contributors in creating unstable plaque, as depicted in Figure 2.2. Moreover, these factors can be measured and actively managed, through lifestyle and improved nutrition, and when necessary, with medications and dietary supplements.

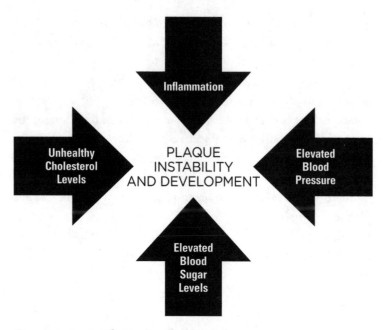

Figure 2.2: Factors affecting plaque build up and ruptures.

All too often though, people look at one condition alone, such as controlling high blood pressure or cholesterol. But each of these factors interact and can have a profound influence on the others. Unhealthy cholesterol levels are more of a problem when accompanied by high levels of inflammation. High blood sugars have been found to be inflammatory and cause unfavorable changes in cholesterol levels. High blood pressure damages the inner lining of the artery, giving cholesterol the opportunity to do harm. High levels of inflammation, in turn, can make cholesterol even more damaging.

The Cholesterol Factor

Contrary to popular belief, cholesterol is essential for human life. It is an important component of each cell wall. Cholesterol is used in the body's synthesis of the male and female reproductive hormones. It is also a building block of bile, the agent essential for digesting essential fats and supporting the absorption of many important vitamins. Approximately 70-80 percent of the cholesterol found in the bloodstream is produced in the body. Only a small portion comes from food.

Cholesterol does harm when it penetrates the inner lining of the artery, the endothelium, and collects beneath this layer. This triggers a series of reactions that results in the development of plaque.

Until the early 1990s, many doctors did not look to manage the different types of cholesterol. Lowering total cholesterol was the objective.

Cholesterol is carried through the blood stream by binding itself to protein. Combined they are known as lipoproteins. The body creates different lipoproteins, each serving different functions. A particular cholesterol carrier, the low density lipoprotein (LDL), has been identified as the primary villain in plaque development and is popularly known as "bad" cholesterol.

The relationship between LDL cholesterol and arterial plaque has been extensively studied. In people that naturally have very high LDL cholesterol, life-threatening levels of plaque have been found fairly early on -- even in the complete absence of other risk factors. Cholesterol-lowering medication may be critically important for the health of these individuals.

LDL cholesterol management also has proven useful in reducing the threats created by other risk factors. Do you have a family history of heart disease unrelated to your LDL cholesterol levels? Have you already been diagnosed with extensive plaque? Has your doctor identified other factors, like high blood pressure that increase your chances for a heart attack or stroke? Are your lifestyle choices, like smoking, physical inactivity, or overeating, putting you at risk?

Reducing LDL cholesterol can offset these other risks. But if you are taking a cholesterol-lowering medication and now think that you are protected from unhealthy lifestyle choices, think again. For those utilizing only statins, the leading cholesterol-lowering medications, to manage cholesterol, the risks of a heart attack decreases by only

30 percent. Seventy percent of the risk remains! Medical science continues to evolve in an effort to close this 70 percent gap.

Starting Cholesterol Management Earlier

Most people wait to address heart health until sometime after age 40. At about this age, the risk of a heart attack or a stroke rises quickly.

Plaque starts building years earlier, often in early adolescence and sometimes during childhood. By 40, we simply have given the plaque building process enough time to reach dangerous levels. And once plaque is established, it can be difficult to remove through lifestyle choice alone. Surgery or other medical procedures may be needed.

The American Heart Association (AHA) recommends that cholesterol levels be checked at age 20. The American Academy of Pediatrics also recently recommended that cholesterol management may even be appropriate for much younger people.[11]

Cholesterol Testing and Children

In 2008, the American Academy of Pediatrics (AAP) revised its policy on cholesterol screening in children based on what it saw as "new urgency given the current epidemic of childhood obesity with the subsequent increasing risk of Type 2 diabetes mellitus, hypertension, and cardiovascular disease in older children and adults." The AAP noted that while most of the burdens of heart disease occur among adults, "research over the last 40 years has increasingly indicated that the process of atherosclerotic CVD [cardiovascular disease] begins early in life and is progressive throughout the life span."[12]

AAP recommends cholesterol screening for:
1.   Children 2 years and older with a family history of

heart disease, high cholesterol, or strokes, or when the child is overweight, has high blood pressure, or diabetes. Screening before 2 years of age is not recommended. If values are within the reference range on initial screening, the patient should be retested in 3-5 years.

2. For children who are overweight and have a high triglyceride concentration or low HDL concentration, the first course of treatment should focus on weight management, improved diets with nutritional counseling, and increased physical activity

3. Cholesterol-lowering medications should be considered for patients 8 years and older with high LDL concentration of 190 mg/dL or more. Medications may also be appropriate at lower LDL levels if other risk factors, like a family history of heart disease, are present.

You may find the prospect of giving children cholesterol-lowering medications alarming. Surely a better solution would be to improve their eating habits and exercise levels!

We certainly believe so. Medications are rarely without risk and always come with a cost. Pediatricians, however, face a challenge. Increasingly they find themselves treating overfed and inactive children. Some may have diabetes or may be pre-diabetic, while others may exhibit very unhealthy cholesterol and blood pressure levels. These children face a growing risk for heart disease and stroke early in life. Absent a major change in the health trends of younger generations, the pharmaceutical tools used to treat the chronic condition of older people will be more widely considered for the young

"Acceptable" Cholesterol Does Not Equal Optimal

You have been told that your cholesterol levels are fine. What does that mean? Rather than indicating good health, this may simply mean that your cholesterol levels are not high enough to justify the risks and costs of treatment with medication. In fact, most Americans, including those taking cholesterol-lowering medication, have higher cholesterol levels than considered optimal.

The National Cholesterol Education Program (NCEP), an initiative within the National Institutes of Health (NIH), defines the standards for use of cholesterol-lowering medication (see Figure 2.3). Along with the dangers associated with high cholesterol, the NCEP researchers consider the risks associated with taking the drug as well as the cost of the drug's use for both the individual and society. They issue recommendations through a lengthy and extensive evaluation process. Doctors and insurance companies use these recommendations to guide treatment. Periodically these guidelines are updated based on new information and the availability of new medicines or technologies.

Cholesterol Targets as Defined by NCEP			
CHOLESTEROL TYPES			
	TOTAL	LDL	HDL
Desirable	<200		>60
Borderline	200-239		40-59
Undesirable	240+		<40
Optimal		<100	
Near Optimal		100-129	
Borderline High		130-159	
High		160-189	
Very High		190+	

Figure 2.3 NCEP Cholesterol Targets

Under the current NIH guidelines, LDL cholesterol targets vary according to individual risks including family history, smoking, diabetes, and levels of HDLs. If you have no other risk factors, you may not be a candidate for medications if your LDL levels are less than 160mg/dl. If you have some risk and cholesterol below 130mg/dl, you still may not be prescribed medications. In each of these cases, the untreated LDL cholesterol remains above the optimal level.

A wide gap remains between the healthiest cholesterol levels and the levels at which medications are routinely recommended. Does this mean that more people should be taking cholesterol-lowering medications? Some doctors do prescribe these medications more intensively than recommended by the NCEP. We look to the incredible power of heart healthy eating and other lifestyle improvements to bring cholesterol to the more optimal levels while also addressing other factors creating unstable plaque.

The simple fact remains — everyone with LDL cholesterol levels above the optimal levels can improve their health and wellness by bringing them down!

Not All LDLs Are Created Equally Harmful

Just as the early focus on total cholesterol proved inadequate, a focus on total LDL levels proves inadequate. Certain LDL subcategories of LDL particles are more harmful than others. Generally, these are the smaller, denser LDL particles that may more easily penetrate the endothelium, the inner lining of the arteries. These smaller LDL particles also may be more prone to cause greater damage in the presence of inflammation.

Tips from the Cooking Cardiologist – Cholesterol Management

Your total cholesterol should be 100 plus your age. The best way to keep cholesterol from doing damage to the arteries is to take preventative action when you are younger. Rather than considering cholesterol as something that needs to be dealt with when you're older, it's best to understand that the longer you live with elevated levels, the greater the chances for cardiovascular problems. A commitment to heart health early in life is the key to prevention.

Looking Beyond LDLs

LDL cholesterol has gained center stage in efforts to cut heart attacks and strokes for an important reason; proven tools such as medications and lifestyle changes can sharply lower LDL cholesterol levels. However, other, independent factors also play an important role in heart health and disease prevention and include the high density lipoproteins (HDL). Where LDL cholesterol are the villains, HDL cholesterol are the heroes. Among its functions, HDL (or "good" cholesterol) removes excess cholesterol from the body, taking it to the liver where it can be reprocessed and discarded.

Substantial reductions in LDL cholesterol are often required to significantly lower heart attack risk. Small increases in HDL cholesterol can offer significant improvements. For every 1 percent reduction of LDL cholesterol there is a 1 percent reduction of risk. However with HDL cholesterol, for every 1 percent increase in HDL cholesterol there is a 2 percent reduction of risk. Low HDL cholesterol are most closely associated with the early development of extensive plaque. Low HDL cholesterol levels without elevated LDL cholesterol levels are fairly common. In fact, low HDL cholesterol levels are more common than elevated LDL cholesterol.[13]

The balance between LDL and HDL cholesterol is another important risk factor. If you have acceptable LDL levels, low HDL levels could put you a substantial risk. You also may have elevated LDL cholesterol with very high levels of HDL cholesterol. In these cases, your heart risks may or may not be sufficient to warrant drug treatment.

The Inflammation Factor: The Story Continues

Most people recognize inflammation as the redness, swelling, and pain around an injury. Inflammation is part of the body's efforts to fight infection and heal wounds. It is a crucial mechanism used by the body to survive in hostile surroundings.

But inflammation has its risks. The same process that helps us survive can harm healthy tissues. The human body seeks to tightly control the inflammatory process, turning it on when needed, and then turning it off when not. Sometimes, though, this process burns out of control. Think of controlled inflammation as the fire that burns to keep you warm and cook your foods. Uncontrolled inflammation is the wildfire that destroys healthy forests.

Inflammation alone can be a risk factor for heart disease. You can have low cholesterol levels but still be at higher risk for heart disease if you have high levels of inflammation. The gradual development of plaque leading to a complete blockage is a response to inflammation in the arteries. The development of unstable plaque that can quickly lead to a heart-stopping blockage also is associated with the inflammatory process.

Inflammation can be measured much like cholesterol. The most frequently assessed measure of inflammation is C-reactive protein (CRP). The blood test taken at your most recent physical probably includes your CRP levels.

The chemistry around the role of inflammation and plaque is not entirely understood and is still the subject of much research, but cholesterol does more damage in an inflammatory environment.

The body's ability to regulate inflammation is affected by a number of factors. The stress created by the pulsating flow of blood through the arteries can cause an inflammatory response, particularly at points where the artery might take a sharp turn. These stress points can be found in the major arteries in the heart.

Some foods fuel the inflammation process. Others help "cool" it. Antioxidants, discussed in Chapter Five, can be helpful in supporting the body's own processes to turn off the inflammatory process.

The modern American diet is increasingly inflammatory and delivers fewer of the cooling nutrients, such as antioxidants found in whole plant-based foods. And like high blood pressure and diabetes -- two other conditions closely associated with the foods we eat -- high cholesterol itself is associated with elevated levels of inflammation. Other environmental factors such as smoking and pollution play a role in igniting and feeding inflammation.

Statins: A Multipurpose Class of Medications

Statins are known by their brand names, such as Lipitor and Crestor as well as generics like simvastatin and atorvastatin.

Today, statin sales exceed every other class of drugs, including antibiotics and medicines for diabetes, high blood pressure, and cancer treatment. At last count, sales of cholesterol-lowering medications exceeded $35 billion and counting.

Statins are multipurpose medications, lowering levels of LDLs and inflammation in the arteries. These medications have reduced the number of heart attacks. Heart healthy eating, however, affects cardiovascular risk through more than a dozen different ways, including effects on insulin resistance, endothelial function, and other cholesterol particles. Similarly, statins cannot offset the wide ranging impact of heart harmful eating.

As effective as they are, statins only partially offset the risks of heart disease. Statins are one tool best used in support of a healthy lifestyle.

High Blood Pressure — Another Piece of the Puzzle

High blood pressure affects approximately 25 percent of the adult population worldwide. As traditional diets give way to modern ones and as the world population ages, its prevalance will continue to escalate. In the United States, nearly 130 million or 2 out of every 3 American adults have blood pressure above the healthiest range. About 74 million Americans have hypertension, blood pressure sufficiently high to be classified as a disease.

Unlike veins, which are subject to a lower, more even pressure, arteries routinely face the high pressure, pulsating blood flow from the heart. To some degree, the arteries are made to withstand this pressure. Veins are not.   Each week, for example, thousands of Americans undergo coronary bypass surgery. A healthy, clean vein from another part of the body is brought to the heart where it is used to bypass the blocked artery.   In a few years, however, the replacement vein also becomes thickened, scarred, and riddled with plaque. An example is former President Bill Clinton, whose bypass had to be held open with a "stent" less than ten years from the date of his surgery.

It can take several decades for arteries to become similarly affected. Many people's arteries can withstand the pulsating pressure for a lifetime.

High blood pressure intensifies the natural stress on the arteries, increasing the prospects for the formation of plaque. When blood pressure is measured, two readings are taken. Systolic blood pressure is measured when the heart beats; diastolic blood pressure is measured between heart beats. Blood pressure numbers are written with the systolic number above or before the diastolic, such as 120/80.

Like cholesterol, the NIH sets standards for blood pressure. Blood pressure can be too low. Known as hypotension, it results in an insufficient flow of blood to all parts of the body. Symptoms include dizziness, lightheadedness, headaches, and shortness of breath.

Normal systolic blood pressure should be less than 120mmHg; diastolic should be between 70-80mm of mercury. Systolic pressure above 140 and diastolic pressure above 90 is considered hypertentive,   levels classified as a disease often requiring drug treatment. The blood pressure levels of many Americans falls between the healthy and diseased levels. They are pre-hypertensive. At these levels, you may not be prescribed blood pressure lowering medications. Your doctor may even indicate that you area "fine" but that you should be taking steps to lower your blood pressure, such as lowering the intake of salt. But you should recognize that fine is not necessarily healthly. Even at the pre-hypertensive level, your arteries are still under increased stress.

Category	Systolic, mmHg	Diastolic, mmHg
Low Blood Pressure (hypotension)	< 90	< 60
Normal	90 – 120	and 60 – 80
Prehypertension	121 – 139	or 81 – 89
Stage 1 Hypertension	140 – 159	or 90 – 99
Stage 2 Hypertension	≥ 160	or ≥ 100

Blood Sugar, Cholesterol, and Inflammation

The human body has evolved to carefully regulate the levels of sugar in the bloodstream. When sugar levels fall, the appetite is triggered. When they rise, insulin is released into the blood.

The insulin enables the cells to metabolize the sugar. When the level of sugar exceeds the body's needs for energy, the body seeks to store it. Sugar is first converted into glycogen that can be stored in the muscles, available for quick use. When the storage capacity of the muscles is reached, the sugars convert to triglycerides, a fatty acid stored in the fat cells. This process is very dynamic. After a meal, both blood sugar and triglycerides increase. Blood sugar can rise very quickly, triggering a release of insulin as well as the process that coverts the sugars to stores of energy — glycogen and triglycerides — that can be used later. Triglycerides in the blood can start to rise in two hours but typically not later than six hours after a meal. After eight hours without eating, the triglycerides will drop back down to the pre-meal level.

Before meals were oversized and when people burned more calories and consumed more fiber and fewer processed foods, blood sugar levels rose more slowly. Blood sugar and triglycerides also peaked at lower levels. Triglycerides also would fall to lower levels over the course of a day.

Today people consume more and eat easily digestible food, such as sugar and highly processed grains that are quickly absorbed into the blood. Their blood sugar levels rise more rapidly and reach higher levels. Constant grazing on baked goods, processed snack foods, sugar-laden soft-drinks, or juices results in consistently high blood sugar levels. The body, in turn, looks to continue releasing insulin into the bloodstream.

Over time, the cells might become insulin resistant. This situation verges on diabetes – not because the system lacks insulin, but because the cells have become desensitized to the affects. The impact on heart and arterial health are considerable. Diabetics, for instance, are 2-3 times more likely to develop cardiovascular disease.[14] Even with medication, the diabetic individual cannot regulate blood sugar within the tight ranges achieved in a healthy person. The full impact of blood sugar levels and heart health are not entirely understood, but we do know that the elevated blood sugar levels contribute to higher levels of inflammation within the arteries.[15] High levels of triglycerides also are inversely related to "good" HDL cholesterol. When triglycerides go up, HDL levels go down.

The adverse impact of elevated blood sugar levels starts well before diabetes is diagnosed. More Americans have become pre-diabetic (see Figure 2.4). Their ability to control blood sugar has declined, but not so much so that they are classified as diabetics.

Plasma Glucose Result (mg/dL)	Diagnosis
Mid-80s	Target
99 or below	Normal
100 to 125	Pre-diabetes (impaired fasting glucose)
126 or above	Diabetes*

Figure 2.4 Blood Sugar Levels and Diabetes

Elevated triglycerides, lowered HDLs, increased inflammation, and a declining ability to regulate blood sugar add up to a condition known as metabolic syndrome or Syndrome X, a combination of medical disorders that increase the risk of developing cardiovascular disease and diabetes. Today, metabolic syndrome is a growing risk factor for heart attacks and stroke.[16]

Metabolic Syndrome

The American Heart Association and the National Institutes of Health now recognize a combination of risk factors under its own name, metabolic syndrome. Three or more of the following are used to diagnosis this syndrome:

- Elevated waist circumference:
  - Men — Equal to or greater than 40 inches (102 cm)
  - Women — Equal to or greater than 35 inches (88 cm)
- Elevated triglycerides:
  - Equal to or greater than 150 mg/dL
- Reduced HDL ("good") cholesterol:
  - Men — Less than 40 mg/dL
  - Women — Less than 50 mg/dL
- Elevated blood pressure:
  - Equal to or greater than 130/85 mm Hg
- Elevated fasting glucose:
  - Equal to or greater than 100 mg/dL

An Attack on All Fronts

Many of our lifestyle choices move us from low-risk to high-risk for heart disease. Eating choices and lower levels of physical activity can cause high blood pressure, metabolic syndrome and diabetes, high levels of inflammation, and unhealthy cholesterol levels. When these factors interact, even greater harm can be done.

In 2010, the Centers for Disease Control (CDC) reported that 45 percent of adult Americans have hypertension, elevated cholesterol or diabetes.[17] Increasingly, individual Americans face two or three of these conditions. Figure 2.5 illustrates these alarming statistics.

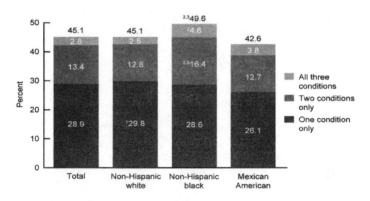

Figure 2.5. Prevalence of Hypertension, Hypercholesteromia, and Diabetes in Adults by Conditions and Race/Ethnicity

The lifestyle challenges to the health of the American heart is more extensive than even the CDC study suggests. The ranges defined for healthy, pre-diseased, or diseased all are somewhat arbitrary. They are simply ways to categorize conditions and provide a framework for medical treatment.

Increasingly, millions of Americans, young and old alike, find themselves at the pre-disease levels for blood sugars, blood pressure, or high cholesterol. Heart attack and stroke risk rise as each of these factors move away from the healthier levels.

"This is a clear, present, and preventable danger," said Dr. Alok K. Gupta at the 2010 meeting of the American Society of Hypertension.[18]

Dr. George Bakris, a professor of medicine and the director of the Hypertension Center at the University of Chicago, put it this way: "If you have pre-diabetes, it's the fire, and pre-hypertension is the gasoline that's added to the fire."[19] Add even somewhat elevated LDL cholesterol -- below the point where medication may be indicated but above the levels considered optimal -- and the fire can rage.

Chapter 3
MANAGING YOUR RISK

First, the bad news: Americans find themselves at increasing risk for heart disease, and more than one out of three will die from heart disease or stroke. Despite a drop in smoking—a leading risk factor for heart disease — only 7.5 percent of Americans are at low risk for heart disease, down from 10.5 percent from the late 1980s. Many who had previously been at low risk have moved to moderate risk, while those at moderate risk are now high risk.[20]

Death rates alone cannot describe the burden of heart disease and stroke. The cost of cardiovascular diseases in the United States exceed $500 billion in 2010.[21] As the U.S. population ages, the economic impact of cardiovascular diseases on our nation's health care system will become even greater.

The good news is that the death rate is declining. While the leading cause of death remains heart disease, the rate was 66 percent lower in 2006 than in 1950. The death rate from stroke, the third leading cause of death, dropped 76 percent. Modern medicine has achieved huge improvements in the ability to treat and prevent a "cardiovascular event" like a stroke or heart attack. A consistent flow of new drugs and medical techniques allows doctors to save lives. But hold the applause. The American heart is no healthier, and perhaps sicker, than it was in the 1950s. We are just building better ambulances and hospital treatments to manage the heart attack or stroke.

Here's the best news of all: We increasingly understand how to prevent and reverse heart disease through healthier eating and healthier lifestyles.

Modern Medicine Working to Keep Pace

More and more, doctors are able to act before a heart attack or stroke occurs. Through various technologies, they can determine whether arteries are narrowed. When the artery in the heart is at risk of closing, a cardiologist might thread a tube from the artery in the arm or leg into the heart, widening the artery. The cardiologist can also insert a "stent" to hold the artery open. If the situation is more critical, a surgeon can perform open heart surgery. In this procedure, the surgeon bypasses one or more diseased arteries in your heart, replacing them with a vein from another part of your body.

Modern medicine also has tools to slow or prevent the development of life-threatening heart disease. Over the past twenty years, the use of cholesterol-lowering medications has increased tenfold among Americans ages 25-65, from 2 to 22 percent.[22] During the same twenty years, the number of Americans taking diabetes medications increased 30 percent. Almost one in three adults -- about 70 million Americans-- has high blood pressure. In 1988, only about 27 percent kept it under control. By 2007-08, that number climbed to 50 percent, largely through the increased use of medication.[23]

The tools available to doctors – early detection, medications, medical procedures and surgery, more medications – all improve the odds for preventing and surviving a heart attack.

This success, however, marks a profound shift for medicine. We once looked to medicine to address illnesses outside our control, such as infections caused by bacteria and viruses. These also include cancer, diabetes, and heart issues that even the most health-conscious may face. Increasingly though, we look to medicine to protect us from bad habits and save us from ourselves. We are building a bigger, better Band-aid to treat the conditions created by our own choices!

First Steps to Avoiding a Heart Attack: Assessing Risk

To play an active and informed role in your own heart health, you should understand the risk assessment tools. The review begins with your health profile. Your age and family history of heart disease are some factors outside your control. Your weight, level of physical activity, and smoking history are other important factors that you can seek to manage.

Your blood pressure will be measured. Next, a routine blood test will measure your blood lipid, including – LDL and HDL cholesterol and triglycerides along with blood sugar, and insulin levels. The markers for inflammation, like C-reactive protein (CRP), will also be identified.

As part of a routine physical, you may be given a resting electrocardiogram (EKG) in which electrodes are attached to your chest and limbs while you lie quietly on a table. As your heart beats, electrical impulses are sent out. The EKG tracks these impulses and identifies abnormal rhythms that can signify heart damage and abnormal heart rhythms.

Depending on the results of these tests and your health profile, you also might be given a stress test. This involves being attached to the EKG while using a treadmill. The stress test can identify diminished blood flow to some parts of the heart. If the blockage is identified, an angioplasty or bypass surgery may be needed.

Stress tests are effective and a very good indicator of heart disease, but often fail to predict a heart attack or stroke. As noted in Chapter Two, it takes at least 75 percent narrowing of a coronary artery to fail a stress test. What is frustrating is that heart attacks can occur when arteries are less than 50 percent narrowed. That is why "Harry" can pass his stress test today and have "the big one" tomorrow. The stress test cannot assess the presence of unstable plaque.

Heart Health Assessment for Women

For women, EKGs are often problematic. The EKG more frequently can suggest a problem with the heart when none exists and may fail to suggest an issue when it does.

The cause is unknown, but we think that the coronary blockages in the women's arteries tend to affect the micro blood vessels, not the larger arteries.   The solution: women should always have imaging of their heart with any stress test.

There are some other important difference in the way heart disease affects women compared to men:

- The most common warning sign of a heart attack in both men and women is chest discomfort - most heart attacks involve discomfort in the center of the chest that last more than a few minutes, or that goes away and comes back. It can feel like uncomfortable pressure, squeezing, fullness or pain. Women, however, are somewhat more likely than men to experience other symptoms, particularly shortness of breath, nausea or vomiting, and back or jaw pain.

- Since women tend to have heart attacks later in life than men do, they often have other diseases (such as arthritis or osteoporosis) that can mask heart attack symptoms. Increased age and the more advanced stage of coronary heart disease in women can affect treatment options available to physicians. Increased age also can help explain women's greater mortality after heart attacks.

The American Heart Association has launched its "Go-Red-For-Women" campaign to support heart research and education for women. The website is www.goredforwomen.org.

The Next Steps in Predicting a Heart Attack: The Framingham Risk Scores

In 1948, a major research project known as the Framingham heart study was launched by the National Institutes of Health. At that time, little was known about general causes of heart disease, but death rates had been rising since the beginning of the twentieth century.

The researchers recruited 5,209 men and women between the ages of 30 and 62 from the town of Framingham, Massachusetts. They conducted in-depth physical examinations and lifestyle interviews. The subjects returned every two years for a detailed medical history, physical examination, and laboratory tests. In 1971, the study enrolled the next generation -- 5,124 of the original participants' adult children and their spouses -- to take part in similar examinations.

In April 2002, the study enrolled the third generation, the grandchildren of the original participants.

Over the years, the Framingham study has tracked the impact of the major risk factors for heart disease and stroke -- high blood pressure, high blood cholesterol, smoking, obesity, diabetes, and physical inactivity. It also tracked valuable information on the effects of other factors such as triglyceride and HDL cholesterol levels, age, gender, and psychosocial issues.

Risk calculators have been defined from this data and include predicting a 2 and 10 year risk of a first heart attack or stroke. If you have low cholesterol and normal blood pressure, your heart risks are lower. What is low cholesterol? Remember Dr. Collins rule of thumb: for an otherwise healthy person, your total cholesterol should be no more than 100 plus your age, (and if you have heart disease or other serious risks facts, cholesterol levels should be lower (see discussion in Chapter Two).

As total cholesterol, LDL cholesterol, age, and blood pressure rise and as HDL cholesterol levels fall, you may find yourself at intermediate risk; that is, having a 10-20 percent chance of a heart attack over the next 10 years. As these factors continue to worsen, you can become high risk, with at least a 3 in 10 chance of a heart attack. Using the Framingham calculators, you can calculate your own prospect for a heart attack or stroke within the next 10 years.

Case Studies: Rob Leighton and "Jack Jones"

Rob Leighton

When he was in his late 40s, coauthor Rob Leighton ran a specialty chocolate company, grabbing a coffee and bagel during his morning commute and lunching on takeout Chinese or cheeseburgers. His professional wife took care of the morning shift, getting their two children off to school. When he was not on business trips, Rob took the evening shift, cooking what he thought were healthy dinners. With both Rob and his wife working, "slack" time was focused on their kids. He felt somewhat guilty if he took an hour for himself, even for exercise.

A few years earlier, Rob's doctor had told him his blood chemistry, including his cholesterol levels, were "fine." In applying for life insurance, however, Rob was required to take a blood test. This time, however, blood was drawn a few hours after lunch, where in the previous test he'd fasted the night before. And what a shock: His cholesterol had moved into a high-risk range to nearly

251mg/dl; his LDLs was 174mg/dl; his HDLs, 61mg/dl. Under the National Institutes of Health guidelines, he was a candidate for cholesterol-lowering medication.

Rob knew that he had a family history of high cholesterol and stroke, but was really not aware of the significance of the numbers. He was approved for the life insurance. Nearly a year passed before Rob completed another full physical. This time, he had his blood drawn after a 12-hour fast.

The numbers were better. Total cholesterol moved from the undesirable levels into the high borderline range. His LDL levels remained in the high range, but just short of borderline high. Under the NIH guidelines, Rob might still have to take cholesterol-lowering medications. His doctor indicated he should work towards reducing his cholesterol. If the numbers did not improve in the next six months, Rob would need to consider a statin medication.

Rob replaced bad fats with good fats, increasing his intake of certain soluble fibers and started on plant sterols and Omega-3s. He lost a few pounds and exercised more regularly. Overall, he was reasonably compliant with the improvements. Perhaps four out of seven days a week, he met his goals.

Six months later, a blood test showed significant progress. His total cholesterol had fallen to 201mg/dl. More importantly, his LDLs were lowered to 130mg/dl. According to the National Institutes of Health's recommendation, Rob no longer required cholesterol-reducing medication.

In terms of his long-term risk for a heart attack, what had Rob accomplished? He had cut his chances of a heart attack within the next 10 years by 25 percent to a calculated risk of 3 percent; that is, 3 out of 100 people with Rob's age and risk profile would have a heart attack in the next 10 years.

Most doctors would encourage Rob to drive his cholesterol levels even lower. They would recognize that while the cholesterol levels Rob achieved were better, they fell far short of optimizing his heart health. Total cholesterol, they might argue, should be below

150mg/dl. Optimal LDL levels for most should be below 100mg/dl. Lower than 80mg/dl would be even better.

For Rob, and other patients like him, no one course of treatment or formula exists to achieve these more aggressive goals. Some doctors use medications more freely. They see the pain, suffering, and costs of heart and arterial disease on a daily basis. They also may have little confidence in their patients' abilities to change their lifestyles.

Other doctors may have concerns over the known risks of particular drugs and the unknown risks of taking multiple drugs over extended periods of time. They also may be more optimistic that patients will at least partially be successful in making lifestyle changes. They work with their patients to journey toward a substantially healthier lifestyle that can sharply drop heart health risks either without medications or with significantly reduced dosages.

The key point here is that different doctors will choose varying goals for the same individual. Even doctors who agree on goals may prescribe dissimilar treatments. But this is your life and your health. You need to know and track your risks. And you need to take an active role in selecting your course of treatment!

"Jack Jones"

When "Jack Jones" (not his real name) was 59 years old, he weighed 215 pounds and stood 5'10" tall. He exercised about twice a week, 40-minute workouts of medium intensity. Jack liked to eat foods such as organic butter and ice cream, and "natural" potato chips, shopping often at health food stores.

Jack was taking a low dose of the cholesterol lowering medication, Lipitor. His total cholesterol was 193 and his LDL was 121. For otherwise healthy individuals, these cholesterol levels might be considered acceptable, although not optimal. Jack, however, had other risk factors. He had a family history of premature coronary disease. He also suffered from high blood pressure and had an abnormal heartbeat. His HDLs were quite low at 23. Also of great concern were his high level of triglycerides, the primary fat within this blood stream, at 303.

Jack decided to make significant improvements to his lifestyle. Along with increasing exercise from two to five times per week, he reduced calorie intake. He altered his total fat content to 25 percent of his daily calories, with no more than 7 percent being saturated fats. He also tried to consume 35-40 grams of fiber per day, with at least 10 grams coming from cholesterol-lowering soluble fiber. He added 2 grams of plant sterols and 3,000 mg fish oils to his daily diet, According to Jack, he was eating "as few animal products, especially animal fats, as possible and tons of vegetables and beans."

Three years later and 38 pounds lighter, Jack's blood test results revealed tremendous improvements. LDLs were dramatically reduced to 52. His HDLs increased to 44, considered in the healthy range, and his triglycerides dropped to 67.

Jack's blood pressure moved into the normal range and he no longer suffers from heartburn. He feels better than he has in a long time. He admits that life-changing experience has taught him what his body needs to feel its best.

In thinking about his journey, Jack reflects, "The longer I go with good habits, the less I crave the 'bad' things, and the more I prefer and crave the 'good' things." Jack has also learned to prepare and savor vegetarian dishes, although he still misses steak and burgers. "And nothing has replaced ice cream yet."

Advanced Diagnostics: Next Generation Heart Assessment Tools

As discussed, today's standard heart health assessment tools still fail to more specifically identify who is at immediate risk for a heart attack or stroke. When a doctor inputs your risk factors into a Framingham assessment and it determines whether you have a 2, 5, 10, or 20 percent chance of a heart attack over the next decade, it simply informs you of the odds, rather than pinpointing who will or will not be stricken. But this is a life and death gamble.

A stress test can identify some potential problems but these tests fail to detect thousands of heart attacks each year. Many heart attacks and strokes occur in individuals with "normal" cholesterol. Even cholesterol lowering statin medication alone reduces heart attack risk by only 30 percent. Without the use of other tools, 70 percent of the risk remains.

A new series of assessments have been developed to provide clearer insight into the health of your heart and arteries. These tests typically are painless, taking just a few minutes to perform. The information obtained from these assessments allow you to better understand your unique risks and more carefully target and highlight the most important lifestyle changes and medication use. Follows are a few readily available tests that will help you and your doctor assess your unique risk.

The Heart Scan (Coronary Calcium Scan)

A heart scan identifies the level of plaque buildup in the heart by looking for specks of calcium in the walls of the arteries. The heart scans essentially are complex X-rays of the beating heart. The images created through the scan show whether you are at increased risk for a heart attack before other signs and symptoms occur. Evidence of calcium in these arteries is also a clear indication of early stage plaque development in other areas.

If no calcium deposits are found in your arteries, your chance of having a heart attack in the next five years is low. If calcifications are found in your heart arteries, your risks are higher. The more calcium found, the higher the risk.

While fairly inexpensive, heart scan use has been limited. Those already at high risk will already be starting more intense treatment and also may undergo even more extensive testing. The heart scan information is thus not likely to provide information that would result in a change in the treatment.

The heart scan is more useful in gauging risks for those without symptoms of heart disease but have some risk factors. Along with the standard heart risk assessment tools, the heart scan can help guide prevention strategies.

Heart scans do have a drawback. Each scan exposes the patient to substantial radiation from xrays, contributing to an increased risk of cancer.

Carotid Artery Ultrasounds

The carotid arteries are the two major arteries channeling the flow of blood from the heart to the brain. Since these large arteries are close to the surface of the skin, their health can be assessed through an ultrasound, known as a CMIT Test, which uses sound waves instead of radiation to create an image. Thus, the carotid ultrasound is a safe and noninvasive way of identifying narrowing in the these arteries -- an important indicator of increased risk for stroke. The carotid arteries also can be used as an indicator of the health of the arteries throughout your body.

Advanced Blood Testing

Beyond routine cholesterol testing, additional blood tests help identify risks associated with cholesterol levels. Advanced tests can look more deeply into components of blood lipids. For example, not all LDL cholesterol is created equal. Among the multiple LDL subclasses floating through the blood are the smaller, denser ones associated with a higher degree of risks. Similarly, not all HDL particles are equally beneficial. The larger HDL particles are the therapeutic work horses and more able to pick up and remove excess cholesterol from the arteries.

Advanced blood testing also may include screening to pinpoint certain genetic markers associated with higher incidence of heart disease and stroke. Some of these genetic markers also may help identify your response to certain medications.

Utilizing Advanced Testing

The medical community remains divided about the usefulness of the tests. Some question whether the results will change their treatment decisions. Others question the wisdom of adding costs to an already financially overburdened healthcare system. And for many, health insurance will not cover all or a substantial part of these advance tests.

There is a risk-benefit ratio. Prevention does cost dollars. However, an initial expense of finding disease early, before it takes control of a person's life, saves on money spent to treat the illness in the future. So the debate continues.

Based on your motivations and risks, review the possible benefits of these tests with your healthcare team. But remember that standard testing often fails to pinpoint whether a heart attack or stroke may be imminent. Advanced testing can help specify preliminary damage or signs and help you tailor a more appropriate approach to your heart health.

Rob Leighton: Assessing risks

At South Denver Cardiology Associates, Dr. Collins and his team took Rob through a series of advanced tests. The tests revealed both good and bad news. In the heart scan, Rob's heart was shown to be free of calcium. In his preliminary carotid artery ultrasound one of the two carotid artery exhibited a fair amount of thickening, raising his risk for a stroke. His advanced blood tests revealed that he had inherited a gene that put him at higher risk for a heart attack. The same gene indicated that Rob would likely respond very favorably to the use of statin medications.

While his total and LDL cholesterol remained above optimal levels, the profile of his LDL suggested a lower risk for heart disease. "Overall, Rob really needs to be more aggressive at getting his cholesterol down," says Dr. Collins. "I would typically recommend a low dose of a statin, but he should also be able to achieve the same results with a more intensified nutritional program focusing on a plant based diet, some supplements and increased exercise. Rob simply needs to understand that the sooner he starts working on slowing down the plaque building process, the better."

Rob observed "The advanced testing and work with Dr. Collins shifted my attention from cholesterol management to a broader interest in my heart health and wellness. While I started with a few dietary changes and took some effective supplements that brought my cholesterol to 'acceptable' levels, I now recognize that I still have some distance to go."

"A few years ago, I would not believe that I would enjoy eating very differently," Rob continued. "The challenge remains in creating the foods that I love but that also love me, but I am finding that the small changes made over months, even years, are adding up to profound ones. Not only have they influenced my food preferences but I have lost about 20 pounds!"

SECTION II:
THE POWER OF HEART HEALTHY NUTRITION

| Understand Your Risks | Understand the Power of Heart Healthy Nutrition | Create Your Heart Healthy Approach to Eating | Continue A Delicious Journey Toward Heart Health |

Chapter 4
RETHINKING THE MACRONUTRIENT DEBATES

Take a stroll through any grocery store, and you'll see a dizzying array of heart healthy products. Cereals, soups, super-fruit drinks, popcorn, salad dressings, margarines and oils, yogurts, nutritional bars, pastas, even chocolate are among the many food categories with products proclaiming their ability to lower cholesterol and blood pressure, fight inflammation, and control blood sugar levels.

Adding even further to the confusion is the fact that no food or specific nutrient rules in the quest for the healthiest. "Low in sodium" "Low in saturated fat" "No cholesterol" "No trans fats" "High in potassium" "High antioxidants" "With plant sterols" "An excellent source of Omega-3s," and "Contains cholesterol-lowering fiber" are only some of the pronouncements. The vitamin aisle has just about as many supplements claiming similar associations to heart health -- CoQ10, Vitamin E, psyllium, niacin, and red yeast rice among many others.

But while nutritional fads abound, many consumers remain dubious. Some believe health claims made by profit-driven companies are overstated. Others doubt that a single food or nutrient can significantly affect their ability to avoid cardiovascular disease.

Our reluctance to place faith in the power of nutrition to support heart health has another origin. Over the past sixty years, nutritional recommendations associated with the macronutrients -- fats, proteins, and carbohydrates -- have been widely advocated by health and medical experts. After years of trial, some recommendations were found not only to be ineffective but were also proven to be harmful.

One Hundred Years of Heart Disease

From the early 1900s through the 1950s, heart attacks and strokes became the leading causes of death and disability in the United States. While antibiotics, vaccinations, public health initiatives and reductions in occupational hazards helped lower mortality, increased longevity and changing lifestyle patterns contributed to the rising incidence of heart disease.

Starting in the 1950s, Americans were told to purge the saturated fats found in red meat, butter and other whole milk dairy product from their diets. High intakes of these fats were found to be associated with heart disease. Margarine was advanced as an important tool in this effort. Margarine was made from heart healthier polyunsaturated fats. For the next two generations, individuals at risk for heart disease were told to use butter alternatives. Studies then revealed that the hydrogenation process used to make margarine created trans-fatty acids, a type of fat more harmful than the saturated fat it replaced.

No fat and lowfat became popular in the 1980s. Lower total fat levels, not just saturated fats levels, were found to lessen the incidence of cardiovascular disease. With each gram of fat delivering over two times the calories of proteins and carbohydrates, reduced fat intake also could offer the benefit of weight reduction.

An important fact was missed. Something had to replace the fats. In many cases, simple carbohydrates found in sugars, white flours, potatoes, and white rice filled the void. These "bad" carbohydrates triggered rapid rises and then sharp declines in blood sugars. Our bodies then called for more food, leading to increases in appetite and calorie consumption. In the wake of the lowfat wave, Americans found themselves heavier, not lighter. The incidence of metabolic syndrome and diabetes also rose. [24, 25]

Lowfat, high simple carbohydrate eating also did damage to our arterial health. With the increased consumption of simple carbohydrates, HDL (good) cholesterol declined while triglycerides increased. This approach to eating also was found to be inflammatory.[26, 27] It remains a prescription for the development of metabolic syndrome. Overall, lowfat, high simple carbohydrate eating helps set the stage for a more rapid development of arterial plaque.

Through the 1990s, the low carbohydrate diet developed by Dr. Robert Atkins gained momentum. It offered a high fat, high protein approach. Healthy eating was a secondary consideration at best. Weight reduction was the primary focus. While turning the tides on the excessive intake of simple carbohydrates, low carb eaters also avoided many of the plant-based foods that we know are useful for long-term heart health.

Under these low carb diets, people also were told they could eat as much as they wanted so long as they stay away from carbohydrates. Enjoy as much steak, butter, eggs, and bacon as you like so long as you stayed away all carbohydrates including whole grains, many vegetables and fruits.

While some achieved significant weight loss, the diet failed to teach and reinforce healthy eating habits. When people returned to a more normal mix of foods -- and most low carbohydrate dieters do -- unhealthy eating habits continued and many regained the weight, and then some, further burdening their hearts.

Moreover, many of the low carbohydrate, higher fat diets were found to be inflammatory, again creating a more favorable environment for the development of unstable plaque.[28] They also were found to compromise the functioning of the endothelium, the inner lining of the arteries. High levels of fats, particularly saturated fats, have been shown to limit the artery's ability relax and dilate.[29]

The effects are striking. Just a few hours after a high fat meal, medical researchers can measure a significant drop in an artery's ability to widen under stress. A few hours later, the arteries can regain their ability to function. But if you are eating only higher fat meals, your arteries may not return to normal. They may remain narrower and restricted.

As 21st century dawned, Americans developed a new and improved understanding of fats and carbohydrates. The heart healthy benefits of a Mediterranean diet, high in certain kinds of fats, vegetables, and fruits, became more widely recognized. A variety of popular diets arose, most notably the South Beach Diet.[30] Developed by Dr. Arthur Agatston, a cardiologist noted for his pioneering effort for improving early detection tools for heart disease, this diet offered a framework for what many physicians intuitively understood. It recognized that there were "good" and "bad" carbs and that there were both better-for-you fats and harmful fats.

Dr. Agatston took the Atkins diet and modified it from a medical point of view, adding the dimension that you can affect both weight and cardiovascular health through altering not only how much but also what you eat.[31] However, Dr. Agatston's original program was not a longer-term cardiac diet but rather a program developed to drop weight in a safer manner. Yet his staged approach is still difficult, especially the first two weeks. It provides a quick burn, a weight loss reward after a tough beginning. Results are motivating, but again often short-lived.

Fats, Proteins, and Carbohydrates - The Basics

Fat is an energy storehouse. The ability to store energy was critical for survival during periods when the availability of food was much more uncertain. Fat represents the body's efforts to store extra calories for use at a later time. But the world has changed. In our fast food, oversized, ready-to-eat world, consuming excessive calories has never been easier.

Fats have other vital functions. Some fats, known as essential fatty acids, are key factors in countless chemical reactions in the body. The body cannot make these essential fatty acids. They must be consumed as either food or supplements. Deny the body these essential fatty acids, and it will be malnourished.

There are many types of fats. They are broadly classified as saturated fats (SFAs), polyunsaturated fats (PUFAs), and monounsaturated fats (MUFAs). All fat-containing food delivers a mix of all three.

Different subclasses of fatty acids have been identified within each of the categories. For instance, Omega-3s are a type of polyunsaturated fat. Trans fats are also MUFAs or PUFAs. Some fats are healthful, while others are not.

"Bad" fats

Both trans and saturated fats are known as "bad" fats.

Trans fats are heart enemy number one. The body responds to trans fats by increasing LDLs and lowering HDLs.[32] Trans fats also have been shown to promote inflammation within the arteries and reduce the arteries' ability to relax and open. [33, 34] Women with the highest trans fat intake had a 73 percent higher level of C-reactive protein (CRP), a marker of inflammation in the blood stream, than women with low trans fat intake.[35]

Most of the trans fats found in the modern diet are formed through the partial hydrogenation of polyunsaturated vegetable oils. Partial hydrogenation is a process that allows fats which are normally liquid at room temperature to solidify, enabling, for example, the creation of stick margarines. Partially hydrogenated oils offer other benefits for food manufacturers. They are relatively cheap, have longer shelf lives, and can improve the texture -- the mouth feel -- of many foods.

Government has taken action to discourage the consumption of trans fats. In 2006, the Federal government required that levels of trans fats be listed on "Nutrition Facts" found on packaged food labels. State and local governments, such as the city of New York and the state of California, restrict or ban the use of trans fats in restaurants.

Trans fats are also found elsewhere. Naturally occurring trans fats are found in meats and dairy products of cows, sheep, goats, and bison. While the levels found in these food products are low, the amount of trans fat associated with the development of cardiovascular disease is also low. On a per-calorie basis, trans fats increase the risk of cardiovascular disease more than any other macronutrient, with a "substantial increased risk at low levels of consumption" (1-3 percent of total daily calories eaten).[36] In fact, large studies have found that a 2 percent increase in energy intake coming from trans fats has been associated with a 23 percent increase in the incidence of coronary artery disease.[37] Nutrition experts recommend that trans fats are best eliminated from our diets.

High levels of saturated fats can be found in red meats and whole milk dairy products. These fats are heart harmful and increase LDL and HDL cholesterol. For most people, saturated fat increases LDL cholesterol far more than it increases the HDL. Moreover, some studies have found that saturated fats impair the body's natural ability to control inflammation and saturated fats have been associated with higher levels of inflammation.[38, 39] Diets high in saturated fats limit the ability of arteries to open, contributing to elevated blood pressure and other heart risks.[40]

"Good" fats

"Good" fats consist of the monounsaturated fatty acids and the less processed polyunsaturated fatty acids. These fats certainly have been found to be substantially less harmful to the heart than the trans and saturated fats. Some also have shown to have healthful effects.

Monounsaturated fats (MUFAs) reduce LDL levels without raising or lowering good HDL levels. MUFAs also have not been shown to contribute to inflammation. In fact, eating styles such as the Mediterranean diet that contain high levels of monounsaturated fats have anti-inflammatory qualities.[41, 42, 43] Olive, teaseed and canola oils are good sources of monounsaturated fats.

Polyunsaturated fats (PUFAs) have been found to lower both LDLs and HDLs. In general, the medical community believes that the LDL lowering effect outweighs the HDL lowering effect, particularly if the PUFAs replace saturated and trans fats.[44] Corn, soy, safflower, and sunflower oil contain high PUFA levels.

As with good versus bad fats, some of the good fats may be better than others. Polyunsaturated Omega-3s, discussed more extensively in Chapter Five, are widely touted for their heart healthful, anti-inflammatory benefits while polyunsaturated trans fats are harmful.

Figure 4.1 describes how "good" and "bad" fats can affect cholesterol levels.

Good Fat / Bad Fat for Cholesterol Management			
Dietary Fat/ Cholesterol	Main Source	State at Room Temperature	Effect on Cholesterol Levels
Total Fat			
Monounsaturated Fat Better	Olive, canola, walnut, almond, avocado, peanut oils.	Liquid	Lowers LDL; No Change in HDL
Polysaturated Fat Good	Corn, soybean, safflower, and cottonseed oil; fish	Liquid	Lowers LDL, Lowers HDL
Saturated Fat Bad	Whole milk. butter, cheese, and ice cream; red meat; chocolate; coconuts, coconut oil	Solid	Raises both LDL & HDL
Trans Fat Worst	Stick margarines; vegetable shortening; partially hydrogenated vegetable oil; many processed foods	Solid or Semi-Solid	Raises LDL, Lowers HDL
Cholesterol - Bad but not as bad as Saturated & Trans Fat	Eggs, non-skim dairy, fatty red meat	N/A	Raises LDL, Raises HDL

Figure 4.1. Good Fat, Bad Fats, and Cholesterol Management

Good Fat versus Lowfat — Reflections of the Cooking Cardiologist

Over my career, some of what we know about fats and the healthy heart has remained the same. We have long understood that significant levels of saturated fats can do harm to arteries and that monounsaturated and polyunsaturated fats are healthier. All fats and oil are energy dense, contributing lots of calories to foods.

We also have gained some added insights. Trans fats resulting from hydrogenizing healthier oils for processed foods causes real harm. Omega-3s, particularly those derived from the sea, support the arterial health. Subjecting all oils, good and bad, to temperatures higher than their smoke point creates compounds that can harm the arteries. Follows are my rules for enjoying fats and oils:

- Enjoy the fats and oils when part of whole, plant-based foods like nuts, seeds, olives and avocados or from fish and shellfish.
- When the fats are separated from the whole foods, use with care. Remember, the healthier oils alone will not make you healthier; but they will make you fatter.
- Use healthier oils to make healthy foods more delicious.
- Using cooking techniques that minimize the amount of oil that you need.

Proteins: Some at Every Meal, Avoid Too Much

Protein is the major structural component of all cells and functions as enzymes and hormones. Protein is one of the major macronutrients and an important source of calories.

Amino acids are the building blocks of protein; many are manufactured by the body. Good health requires about 20 different amino acids. Nine are deemed essential amino acids that must be obtained from food. If all amino acids are not present in the right balance, the body's ability to use protein will be affected. If amino acids needed for protein synthesis are limited, the body may break down body protein to obtain needed amino acids. Protein deficiency affects all organs.

Adequate levels of protein levels may have other benefits. Compared with consuming sugars and other simple carbohydrates, protein helps control appetite.[45] Protein slows digestion and decreases the speed at which sugars are absorbed into the blood stream. Compared with consuming fats, they are lower in calories. Higher protein levels also have been associated with a faster metabolic rate, helping burn calories and resulting in possible weight loss.[46]

Adequate protein also is particularly essential for growth and development for children and young adults. Consumption of animal products easily provides all the essential amino acids needed to build necessary proteins. To achieve the full mix from plants alone, a combination of plant-based foods is often necessary.

But are high protein diets healthier?

When higher protein levels replace unhealthy fats and unhealthy carbohydrates, the diet may be healthier, but as you will learn later in this chapter, not the healthiest. Healthier eating builds on whole, nutrient rich vegetables, beans, fruits and whole grains.

Most Americans, in fact, eat more protein than their bodies need. A focus on further increasing protein can restrict the intake of healthful foods that provide essential nutrients. High protein diets may not offer the variety of foods needed to adequately meet nutritional needs. Some high protein diets, also high in animal-based foods, may elevate the intake of heart harmful saturated fats and dietary cholesterol. Exchanging red meat proteins for plant proteins such as soybeans, peas, and other legumes has benefits. This exchange has been found to lower both cholesterol and blood pressure.[47, 48]

However, while less harmful, increasing the levels of plant, fish, or nonfat dairy proteins, can still increase inflammation, although not as much as red meat proteins. Restricted protein intake lowers inflammation, while increased protein intake can raise inflammation. [49, 50, 51]

Adequate intakes of protein, about 15-20 percent of total calories, is essential for good health. This means that if you are targeting 2000 calories per day, 15-20 percent equates to 75-100 grams of protein. That is about 3-3.5 ounce of protein. Higher intakes, however, offer little intrinsic additional benefit and may contribute to increasing inflammatory levels. But remember: eat some protein at every meal. It has been shown to help reduce the appetite later in the day while raising your metabolic rate. Both these factors can help you maintain your weight.

Looking to Higher Levels of High Quality Carbs

Based on the chemical structure of food and how quickly sugar is digested and absorbed, carbohydrates are categorized as either simple or complex. Complex carbohydrates provide a longer period of feeling satisfied after a meal. The energy in these carbohydrates is more slowly absorbed into the blood stream. Simple carbohydrates can cause a rapid rise in blood sugar levels.

Sugars are simple carbohydrates, easily digested. Fibers cannot be effectively digested by the body and are considered complex carbohydrates. Between simple carbohydrates and fibers are starches. The digestibility of starch varies. Starches found in raw grains, for instance, are complex carbohydrates, difficult to digest, and contribute few calories. Cooked and processed starches are more easily digested and are transformed into simple carbohydrates. When food was scarcer, cooked and processed starches had advantages by making calories more readily available for absorption and use.

Around the world, cooked starches are the foundation of most diets. Rice, wheat, corn, potatoes, and cassava remain essential in feeding the world's populations. In fact, more people eat a plant-based starch diet than any other. Another important benefit is that plant-based diets are much more sustainable than the animal-based diets, requiring a vastly lower amounts of our economic resources, notably land and energy, to generate the same caloric value.

Complex carbohydrates are more than brown rice, whole wheat flour, and other unprocessed grains. Vegetables and beans are a good combination of mostly complex carbohydrates, some protein, a limited amount of fats, and dense in a wide array of other nutrients. While high in sugar, most fruits also contain more complex carbohydrates. The fiber content of the fruit works to slow the absorption of sugar.

Great nutrition starts with mostly complex carbohydrates from less processed foods. Simple carbohydrates can be delivered in moderation and in such a way to make great nutrition more delicious.

Approaches to Counting Carbs

Take a look at the "Nutrition Facts" on packaged foods. Among many other components, the panel lists the total grams of carbohydrate and its components, notably sugars and fibers. There may also be a listing for sugar alcohols like maltitol, xylitol, lactitol, or erythritol. These components of carbohydrates rarely add up to the total. The difference is mostly starch.

Always read these facts panels, especially the fine print identifying serving size and calories. In general, the "Nutrition Facts" are based on a single serving. In any package, there may be two, three or, in many cases, more servings. All too often, people end up eating the whole package, thinking they've only consumed the small amount that defines a single serving.

The glycemic index (GI) and net carbohydrates may be helpful identifying good carbohydrates. The glycemic index is a direct measurement of how quickly a carbohydrate will cause a rise in blood sugar levels. Glucose is 100 on this index. A baked potato is 85. Table sugar, or sucrose, is 65. Fructose, or the sugars found in fruits, are 20. Most beans are in the 30s. The glycemic index of nuts fall in the teens and twenties.

Foods that cause rapid increases in blood sugars, natural or processed, are defined as high glycemic, and have a GI of more than 70. Those with sugars that are more slowly absorbed are low glycemic, with a GI of less than 55. A GI of 54-69 is known as medium glycemic.

The GI fails to consider the amount you eat. The more you eat, the more your blood sugar will rise. Some eating plans thus utilize the glycemic load (GL), a ranking system for carbohydrate content based on their glycemic index (GI) and the portion size, combining both the quality and quantity of carbohydrate into a single number. A high glycemic index food consumed in small quantities may have same effect on blood sugar as bigger quantities of a low glycemic index food.

The impact of even the most highly glycemic foods can be reduced when consumed with fibers, fats, or proteins. So when coupled with a heart healthy meal, a small but wonderful dessert may do little to drive up your blood sugar.

The low carbohydrate dieting community also has incorporated the understanding of good carbs and bad. It has developed the term net carbohydrates for identifying better-for-you carbohydrates.[52] Much like the glycemic index, net carbohydrates are used when comparing foods. Foods with low net carbs are likely to have a low glycemic index. Unlike a GI which specifically measures the speed at which a food affect your blood sugar, the net carbohydrate calculation is based on widely available nutritional data and starts by looking at the total carbohydrates found in a food serving. The components of carbohydrates that only nominally affect blood sugar levels, such as the fiber and a class of lower-calorie sweeteners known as sugar alcohols, are omitted.

Heart healthy eating involves much more than focusing on restricting the impact on blood sugars. Low net carb, low glycemic foods can lack nutrients important to heart health. They also may deliver heart harmful saturated fats, sodium, and cholesterol. Processed meats like bacon, sausage, and jerky fall into this category. So might cheese and sugar-free ice cream.

In focusing narrowly on either the glycemic index or net carbs, it's easy to make the same mistake as during the lowfat, no fat days. Lower fat, particularly saturated and trans fats, was considered a healthier, more calorie-conscious way to eat. But it was only part of the story. The power of nutrition lies with the totality of eating choices. You need to keep your sights trained on the whole diet.

Heart Healthy Eating: The Epidemiology

Epidemiologic research, studies comparing the behaviors and health status of large groups, has found that certain traditional approaches to eating provide sharply reduced risks for cardiovascular diseases, heart attacks, and stroke.[53]

The Mediterranean Diet

The Mediterranean diet attained widespread interest as the result of a seven country study – the United States, Finland, Holland, Italy, Yugoslavia, Greece, and Japan – that explored the relationship between diet and the risk of cardiovascular disease.[54, 55, 56] Consistent with the nutritional wisdom of the day, Americans were found to be six times more likely to have a heart attack than the Japanese. The Japanese diets were lower in fats and higher in fish and vegetables.

Surprisingly, the Japanese faced a higher heart risk than those on the small Mediterranean island of Crete. With as much as 40 percent of daily caloric intake coming from fat, the Mediterranean diet challenged the widely held belief that lowfat eating would best advance heart health. The fats, however, were primarily unprocessed and unsaturated and typically found in olives, olive oils, nuts, and seeds. Vegetables and fruits were also central to these eating traditions as were grains. Fish, shellfish, red meat, dairy, and poultry were used in moderation. Herbs and spices, now recognized as powerful antioxidants, were widely utilized, with sweets consumed in small portions. The Mediterranean diet also made room for modest intakes of alcohol, primarily wine.

Tips from the Cooking Cardiologist

The Mediterranean diet involves far more than enjoying lots of extra virgin olive oil; it starts when you get up and guides your eating patterns throughout the day. Here are some guidelines for Mediterranean eating:

- Never eat breakfast without fruit.
- Every meal should have whole grains or vegetables.
- Emphasize fresh and natural, unprocessed foods.
- Enjoy colorful foods; they contain many of the important vitamins, minerals, and other micronutrients that control inflammation and support arterial health.
- Avoid giving animal-based foods a starring role -- they should be supporting players at best -- perhaps even "extras" on the plate.

- Exercise, even a short walk after eating, can improve your blood lipid and sugar levels.

And remember: Feeling full is your body's way of saying that you have eaten too much! Stop eating when you are satisfied, not full.

The China Study

In his widely read book, epidemiologist T. Colin Campbell explored the health benefits of the diet in rural China. [57] Campbell reported that the death rate from heart disease among American men was seventeen times higher than that of rural Chinese men.[58] He further reported that the average cholesterol levels in much of rural China were substantially lower, in some cases nearly one half, of the average levels found in the United States. [59]

Some elements of the rural Chinese diet were similar to the Mediterranean diet. It emphasized high consumption of plant-based foods and a very limited intake of animal foods. However, Campbell found that, unlike the Mediterranean diet, the rural Chinese diet involved much lower intake of all types of fat, about 15 percent of total daily calories. Lower amounts of proteins also were consumed.

The Okinawan Diet

Okinawans living in southern Japan have had some of the longest life expectancies in the world. The Okinawan diet also was found to be very lowfat with small amounts of protein. But the power of the Okinawan diet is defined not only in what this eating style limits. The power also is found in what is eaten.

Complex carbohydrates represented about 90 percent of the calories.[60] Instead of white rice, a simple carbohydrate used as a staple in most of Japan, Okinawans ate sweet potatoes. Compared with rice, these sweet potatoes contain more fiber as well as high levels of antioxidants and potassium. Vegetables were typically eaten at every meal, including breakfast. Soy in the forms of tofu and seaweed, good sources of Omega-3s, were also ingested daily. While fish and pork were part of the menu, about 10 percent of the daily diet consisted of protein and fat. Green tea was regularly consumed, along with moderate daily amounts of rice-based alcohol.

Traditional Greenland Diet

In the 1970s, native populations of Greenland eating a diet blending traditional eating habits with some modern food also were found to have low levels of heart disease. Their diets emphasized fish consumption. Decreased levels of blood cholesterol, triglycerides, and LDL and increased levels of HDL were found. Their diets delivered low levels of saturated fatty acids and high levels of monounsaturated and Omega-3 polyunsaturated fats.[61] Surveys have shown that these diets included about 14 grams a day of Omega-3s, compared to about 0.2 grams per day in the United States. Interestingly, the intake of dietary cholesterol was high.[62]

Beyond the Low Carb/Lowfat Debate

Is one of these diets better than the other? In comparison with the standard American diet, all are associated with dramatic reductions in cardiovascular disease. The following are common elements and differences in macronutrients:

- Fats
  - Total fat is not a defining characteristic across these diets. The traditional Mediterranean and Eskimo diets deliver more fat than the standard American diet. The Asian diets deliver far less.
  - However, low levels of saturated fats were found. Trans fats were virtually absent from these diets.
  - The fats consumed centered on monounsaturated fats and Omega-3 polyunsaturated fatty acids.

- Proteins represented the smallest component of these heart healthy diets, and at levels much lower than many Americans believe is required for good health.
- Carbohydrates - Minimally processed, complex carbohydrates dominate these eating traditions. None of these traditional diets were low carbohydrate. Simple carbohydrates such as sugar, honey, or processed, fiber-poor grains were used, but at low levels.

The chart in Figure 4.2 illustrates the differences and similarities between the diets. With respect to macronutrients, a wide range of eating styles can qualify as heart healthy.

Diet	Mediterranean	Rural Chinese	Okinawan	Eskimo
Nutrient (Percent Total Calories)				
Total Fat	42%	14.5%	1.6%	39%
Saturated Fat	9%	Low	Low	9%
Polyunsaturated Fat (Omega-3s)	4.4%	Low	Low	7% (5%)
Monounsaturated Fats	26.8%	Low	Low	22%
Total Protein	12.5%	10%	5.3%	23%
Total Carbohydrates	43%	76%	93%	38%

Figure 4.2. Comparison of Macronutrients in Heart Healthy Diets

The right mix or balance of macronutrients can work together to decrease risk of heart attack or stroke, prevent disease, and increase vitality while the wrong combination can undermine your health. Each of these traditional eating patterns delivers a heart healthy mix in their own way.

But there is another central lesson to understanding the

heart health promoting power of these diets. They all deliver a wide range of the micronutrients -- the vitamins, the minerals, the antioxidants, and other plant-based compounds -- that support the healthy heart. Any balance of macronutrients, without the right mix of micronutrients, will fall short of being heart healthy.

From here, medical experts advocate differing eating standards. Some argue that no animal products and very restricted levels of fats should be consumed.[63] Others make room for somewhat higher levels of good fats coupled with limited amount of lean meats, fish, and nonfat dairy products.[64] Still others find room for all varieties of delicious foods so long as they are eaten in moderation and in balance with healthier foods.[65]

What is the right answer? Again, as long as you are building toward a plant-based foundation high in complex carbohydrates and micronutrients, the solution lies with your particular risks. Upcoming chapters will discuss strategies to help you learn why every meal counts, how to match and cook foods to create a healthier balance, and how to develop flexible recipes that you can enjoy today but can adapt to heart healthier eating.

Moving in the Wrong Direction

While we now understand a plant-based foundation, high in complex carbohydrates from vegetables and whole grains, forms the basis for heart healthy eating, our food supply marches in another direction.

For each man, women and child in the United States, the American food supply chain delivers about 30% more calories in 2008 than it did in 1970. No surprise that people are getting heavier. What is striking is how the food supply is changing. It is definitely moving in the wrong direction!

- While Americans are consuming more, the availability of vegetables has remained flat over the period. Produce departments in grocery stores may have expanded, but more vegetables have not been added to the food supply. One explanation is that we have simply swapped frozen and canned vegetables for fresh vegetables. Strikingly, vegetables now represents a significantly smaller *percent* of the supply of foods.

- Fruit supply grew by about 20 percent from 1970-90, but has basically remained flat since then and now represent a declining percentage of the supply of food available.
- Meat, eggs, and nuts have remained essentially flat over the same time period, and like fruits and vegetables, represent a smaller percentage of the total supply of food
- For each person, sugar and other sweeteners did grow over the time period, but this growth has stalled since the early 1990s. What may be true is that one segment of Americans have switched to the artificial, non-caloric sweeteners while other segments have significantly increased their intake of sugar and other sweeteners.

	Food Supply Growth by Category (in Calories)		
Category	1970-1990	1990-2008	1970-2008
Dairy & Other Dairy Fats	171%	103%	175%
Fruit	120%	102%	123%
Vegetables	101%	97%	98%
Meat, Eggs, Nuts	98%	106%	104%
Flour & Cereal Products	133%	109%	145%
Sugar & Other Sweeteners	111%	103%	114%
Added Fats & Oils	111%	138%	153%
Total	117%	111%	130%

Source: Compiled from Preliminary Report of the Dietary Guidelines Advisory Committee on the Dietary Guidelines for Americans, June, 2010.

% of Calories in Food Supply – United States			
Category	1970	1990	2008
Dairy & Other Dairy Fats	7.8%	11.4%	10.5%
Fruit	3.5%	3.5%	3.3%
Vegetables	6.1%	5.2%	4.6%
Meat, Eggs, Nuts	22.5%	18.8%	18.0%
Flour & Cereal Products	21.0%	23.8%	23.4%
Sugar & Other Sweeteners	19.6%	18.6%	17.2%
Added Fats & Oils	19.6%	18.6%	23.0%

Source: Compiled from Preliminary Report of the Dietary Guidelines Advisory Committee on the Dietary Guidelines for Americans, June, 2010.

So where have most of the added calories come from? Added fats and oils, flour and cereals, and dairy products.

So, is the next step simply about finding a better balance among good carbohydrates, good fats, and good protein? No! While Americans may continue their low carb versus lowfat versus high protein debates, they overlook a very important factor. The data indicates that vegetables and fruits are becoming a smaller percentage of our overall diets. While we are eating more, our diets are becoming increasingly unbalanced.

So cast aside the macronutrient debates and focus on building eating patterns around a plant-based diet. This is not about being vegetarian or vegan but rather thinking about how fruits, vegetables, and whole grains define the foundation of what you eat. Meat, dairy, added sweeteners, and oils can make this foundation more delicious and appealing. Again, as long as you are building toward a plant-based foundation high in complex carbohydrates and micronutrients, the solution lies with your particular risks.

Chapter 5
MICRONUTRIENTS FOR HEART HEALTH

Adding specific micronutrients to our food supply has proven an effective public health tool for overcoming "diseases of deficiency." Rickets, a weakening of bones, particularly in children, was caused by inadequate levels of Vitamin D. Cod liver oil was an early supplement that overcame this deficiency. Later, Vitamin D was added directly to foods. Pellagra, an epidemic in the American south less than a century ago, was caused by a niacin deficiency. Brewer's yeast, high in this B vitamin, became the early supplement, with niacin later included in foods. Iron to help prevent anemia; folic acid, another Vitamin B, to reduce birth defects; and Vitamin C to prevent scurvy, have also been added. Even salt tablets in the last century were recommended to be included in the diet for those sweating out in the fields.

Today, a simple Vitamin A supplement could prevent blindness among countless children in the developing world. Between a quarter and a half million children become blind every year due to this Vitamin A deficiency.[66]

In the 1990s, Vitamins A, C, and E and folic acid were touted as improving cardiovascular health. It was hoped that these vitamins, taken in large doses, would cool the inflammatory levels in the arteries and in turn, prevent plaque from forming or becoming unstable. While these theories remain sound, the clinical results proved disappointing. At least for promoting heart health, their intake has fallen out of favor.

Nutrients and Their Impact on Conditions

Today the interest in supplements and cardiovascular health has shifted to other nutrients, including high doses of Omega-3, certain fibers, plant sterols, plant-based antioxidants, red yeast rice, CoQ10, Vitamin D, and niacin. Billions of dollars each year are spent on foods and supplements containing these nutrients. This chapter will discuss specific heart healthy nutrients currently supported by strong scientific evidence. Figure 5.1 illustrates how key nutrients can benefit certain conditions.

Key Nutrients for Heart Health							
	Optimized Heart Health Nutrition	LDL Above Target	HDLs Below Targets	Elevated Triglycerides	Blood Pressure Above Targets	Blood Sugar Regulation	Inflammation
Soluble Fibers (Selected)	X	X		X		X	
Plant Sterols		X					
Omega-3's	X		X	X			X
Niacin as Nicotinic Acid		X	X	X			X
Reduced Sodium	X				X		X
Increased Potassium	X				X		X
Antioxidants	X						X
CoQ10	X						
Vitamin D	X						

Figure 5.1 Key Nutrients for Health

Much like medications, results can vary according to the individual. They should be used judiciously rather than a matter of faith, with an eye to specific improvements – cholesterol, blood pressure, blood sugar and inflammatory levels -- to be measured and tracked by you and your health team.

The Cholesterol Blockers: Plant Sterols and Certain Soluble Fiber

Much of the cholesterol in your blood enters when it is absorbed from your digestive tract. The cholesterol found in foods such as eggs, red meat, whole milk, and cheeses finds its way into the blood stream this way. Yet, eliminating all dietary sources of cholesterol has been found to have a modest impact on lowering LDL cholesterol.

Low Cholesterol Diets versus Cholesterol-Lowering Eating

Cholesterol is only found in animal products. Phytosterols, or plant sterols, are found in plants. Become a vegan, and you will eliminate all dietary sources of cholesterol. With the right mix of only plant-based foods and possibly selected dietary supplements, your total and LDL cholesterol levels can fall by 30% and potentially more. But here is what is interesting. The reduction related to the elimination of cholesterol from your diet will account for relatively small portion of the improvement.

Cholesterol-lowering diets bring a range of nutrients together to affect how much cholesterol your body produces, how much your blood absorbs, and how your body might react to and dispose of it. Cholesterol-lowering diets need not be 100% vegan, but they are plant-based.

Your body, in fact, produces most of the cholesterol found in your arteries. Like cholesterol from food, much of the cholesterol produced by your body finds its way into the blood stream through the digestive track. It is part of a complex process through which your liver uses cholesterol to synthesize bile, an enzyme critical for the digestion of fat. The bile is released into the intestines when the body detects the need to digest fat.

Your body is efficient. Once in the digestive tract, much of the cholesterol-rich bile is broken down. This cholesterol now blends with the cholesterol from the meat and dairy products you've eaten. These various sources of cholesterol can then be absorbed into the bloodstream. Bile secretions typically contribute approximately 1,500 mg of cholesterol per day while the average American eats about 200-400 mg per day.

Two nutrients, plant sterols and selected types of soluble fiber, work to reduce the absorption of both sources of cholesterol.

Plant Sterols

The structure of *sterols,* or phytosterols, is very similar to that of cholesterol. In nature, small quantities of plant sterols can be found in wide a range of foods, particularly vegetable oils. The average American's plant sterol intake is about 250 milligrams a day. Vegetarians typically consume 400 milligrams or more.

Phytosterols have been used to lower cholesterol since the 1950s. The early sterols had several shortcomings. Effectiveness was highly variable, and the daily doses were massive by today's standards. Science has since made natural plant sterols more effective.

A variety of foods have been fortified with plant sterols. Through its National Cholesterol Education Program (NCEP), the United States National Institutes of Health recommends 2-3 grams per day of plant sterols to reduce LDL levels. At these levels, plant sterols can deliver up to 15 percent reduction in LDL cholesterol levels without affecting HDL levels.[67] Figure 5.1 illustrates the sterols in certain types of food.

Source of Plant Sterols		
Source	Serving Size	Free Sterols mg (1)
Selected Natural Sources of Plant Sterols		
Almonds	1 Ounce	30
Apple	1 Large	25
Bananas	1 Banana	35
Corn Oil	1 Tablespoon	135
Garbanzo Beans	1 Ounce	10
Olive Oil	1 Tablespoon	31
Peanut	1 Ounce	62
Rice Bran Oil	1 Tablespoon	167
Safflower Oil	1 Tablespoon	62
Sesame Seeds	1 Tablespoon	100
Soybean Oil	1 Tablespoon	35
Spinach	1 Cup	3
Tomato	1 Medium	9
Walnut	1 Ounce	31

Selected Foods Fortified with Plant Sterols		
Kardea Nutrition Bars*	1 Bar	1000
Benecol	1 Tablespoon	450**
Corazonas Tortilla Chips	1 Ounce	400
Minute Maid O. J. Sterols	8 Ounces	1000
Promise Activ Buttery*	1 Tablespoon	1000
Silk Soy Milk with Sterols	8 ounces	400
Smart Balance Heart Spread*	1 Tablespoon	1000
*1000mg of Sterols from 1700mg of Sterolesters		
**Benecol spread contains 850mg (.85g) stanol esters, about 450 (.45g) stanols		
(1) Intake beyond 3g/day of sterols does not appear to results in further LDL reduction.		

Figure 5.1

Select Soluble Fibers

Plants provide two types of fiber: soluble and insoluble. Soluble fibers absorb and dissolve in water, while insoluble fiber cannot. Certain soluble fibers lower cholesterol by preventing its absorption into the blood stream. The beta-glucan soluble fiber in oats and barley helps lower cholesterol. Psyllium husk, more widely used to support digestive health and regularity, is perhaps the most concentrated source of cholesterol-lowering fibers. The soluble fiber in beans and fruit also works to lower cholesterol absorption. The NIH recommends a minimum of 10 grams of soluble fiber per day, about five servings of oatmeal, not an option for most people. For maximum impact, it targets 25 grams per day. At these levels, as much as an 8 percent reduction in cholesterol is achievable. And, while the soluble fber found in barley, oats, psyllium, fruits, and beans reduce cholesterol, not all soluble fibers do. Figure 5.2 illustrates selected sources of soluble fiber that do.

Selected Sources of Soluble Fiber
Source: NIH National Health Lung Blood Institute

Foods	Soluble Fiber (g)	Total Fiber (g)
CEREAL GRAINS (1/2 cup cooked)		
Barley	1	4
Oatmeal	1	2
Oatbran	1	3
SEEDS		
Psylium Husk 1 Rounded Teaspoon	3	4
FRUIT (1 medium fruit)		
Apple	1	4
Bananas	1	3
Oranges	2	2-3
Peaches	1	2
Pears	2	4
Plums	1	1.5
LEGUMES (1/2 cup cooked)		
BEANS		
Black Beans	2	5.5
Kidney	3	6
Lima Beans	3.5	6.5
Navy Beans	2	6
Northern	1.5	5.5
Pinto Beans	2	7
Lentils	1	8
PEAS		
Chick Peas	1	6
Black Eyed Peas	1	5.5
VEGETABLES (1/2 cup cooked)		
Broccoli	1	1.5
Brussel Sprouts	3	4.5
Carrots	1	2.5

Figure 5.2. Sources of Soluble Fiber

Cheerios, Oats, Barley, and Heart Health

General Mills, the manufacturer of Cheerios, once claimed that eating the cereal lowered cholesterol by 4 percent in just six weeks. They printed it on the box and many people believed it to be true – except for the Food and Drug Administration (FDA), who challenged the statement. While such a claim might be supported, a consumer would have to eat three bowls of Cheerios a day for six weeks! So it was later changed to " helps reduce the risk of heart disease," rather than indicating a specific number. The moral of this story: Look beyond a single food to support heart health to the impact of your overall eating patterns.

Oats vs. barley

Oats have their champions. Major brands in the United States -- Cheerios, Quaker Oats, and Kellogg's -- have done an excellent job in educating the public regarding the cholesterol managing benefits of oats. The central beneficial ingredient in oats is the beta-glucan soluble fiber.

Barley delivers just as much of this cholesterol-lowering fiber as oats.

Moreover, barley is low on the glycemic index -- the measure of how foods affect blood sugar levels. Barley slowly releases its energy into the bloodstream, much more slowly than most whole grains, including brown rice and oatmeal.

Properly prepared, barley also is delicious and can complement many dishes, serving as a high fiber substitute for rice, potatoes, and other starches. Where the Spanish have used white rice as the basis of paella for over 500 years, we are using our everyday barley pilaf recipe to build a healthier version of this great dish of Spain.

If barley is so good, why don't more people eat it? At least part of the answer lies with the subtleties of cooking barley. To prevent it from turning into porridge, follow the directions in our barley pilaf recipe in Chapter 9 and be attentive to stirring and fluffing. If you take a bit of care, your barley pilaf can be a great tasting, nutritious alternative to high glycemic, low fiber carbs.

A bowl of oatmeal in the morning is not enough. You need to eat more cholesterol-lowering fiber, and that can be found in barley. Oatmeal in the morning, barley at night.

Omega-3s: All the Rage

Omega-3s are a polyunsaturated fat. Considered essential fatty acids, they occur as alpha-linolenic acid (ALA), primarily in flax, soy, canola oil, and walnuts and as eicosapentanoic acid (EPA) and docosahexaenoic acid (DHA) in fish oils. Malnourishment results without one or more of these Omega-3s from a dietary source, and in fact Omega-3s are now added to infant formulas.

In terms of cardiovascular health, the most beneficial are EPA and DHA. While not found to lower LDL cholesterol specifically, they reduce triglycerides and make LDL cholesterol less harmful. These Omega-3s are also anti-inflammatory.[68]

How important are Omega-3s to cardiovascular health? Studies have indicated that Omega-3s can reduce the risk of a cardiovascular event in a healthy adult by as much as 18-20 percent. For those with a history of heart disease, the impact has been shown to be at least as significant and perhaps greater.[69]

Leading medical organizations have different recommendations for Omega-3s. The American Heart Association and the American College of Cardiology Foundation, for instance, emphasize obtaining these nutrients from fish.[70] Other organizations recognize that some people will require supplementation to attain the target levels.

Target levels Omega-3s with DHA and EPA can be summarized as follows:

- 0.5-2 grams/day of Omega-3s from fish oil for adults who have not been diagnosed with coronary artery disease.

- 1-2 grams/day for adults who have been shown to have coronary artery disease.

- 3-4 grams/day for adults with highly elevated triglycerides.

DHA supplements made from algae also are available for vegetarians.

Omega-3s are now considered so useful for certain conditions that high potency EPA/DHA capsules are now available not only as a dietary supplement, but also as a prescription medication. A new test that can be done at home with a simple finger stick is also available to measure the Omega-3s in your bloodstream. Do you think you are getting enough Omega-3s? Check the website www.omegaquant.com to find out.

But if you are on a blood thinner, even a low dose aspirin, check with your physicians before consuming high levels of fish oil.

Omega-3s from Non-Marine Sources

ALA Omega-3s come from non-marine sources and can be found in flaxseeds and flaxseed oil, canola oil, walnuts, and at lower levels, in soybean and olive oil. The evidence linking ALA to cardiovascular health is less extensive but still significant. The benefits of ALA appears to be related to their anti-inflammatory power. But be cautious. ALA must be converted into the working agents, EPA and DHA, and humans are not effective at doing so -- only 4 percent at most are actually converted. So don't let the supplement and fortified foods fool you. While a fortified food may contain 1,000 mg of Omega-3s, it may be supplemented with ALA which is strongly debated as truly heart protective.

Omega-6 versus Omega-3: A Role in Inflammation?

Omega-6 is another type of Omega polyunsaturated fat (PUFA). Americans are likely to consume high levels of Omega-6s in meats, salad dressings, oils, and nut products. Also an essential fatty acid, Omega-6 is a pro-inflammatory. However, in comparison with other saturated fats and trans fats, PUFAs -- including even Omega-6 -- improve cholesterol levels. And inflammation isn't all bad; the body uses it to support healing of diseased or damaged areas. But inflammation must be controlled to prevent healthy cells from being damaged.

Some nutrition researchers suggest that humans evolved on a diet with a 1:1 ratio of Omega-6 to Omega-3; that is, every time a person consumed a gram of Omega-6, they also ingested a gram of an Omega-3.[71] In Western diets today, the ratio is quite dramatically different -- about 16 Omega-6s to 1 Omega-3.

Today's corn-fed beef, pigs, and chicken have been found to have lower Omega-3 levels than the grass fed animals that used to make up our food supply. Higher levels of Omega-3s can be found in eggs from free-range chickens that eat a wider variety of foods.

Some believe that changes in the ratio of Omega-3s to Omega-6s have resulted in an imbalance between pro- and anti-inflammatory nutrients. According to the theory, the result is an accelerated development of atherosclerosis along with other inflammatory diseases.

To minimize this outcome, some experts advocate a 4:1 ratio between Omega-6s and Omega-3s.[72, 73] Others, however, remain less convinced.

A 2009 report from the American Heart Association Scientific Advisory Board states that while increasing Omega-3 PUFA "levels does reduce the (heart disease) risk, it does not follow that decreasing Omega-6 levels will do the same." While the report recognizes that Omega-6s might have an impact on inflammation, it argues that the effect is quite low. It emphasizes the benefits associated with consuming polyunsaturated fats, particularly as a replacement for saturated fats.[74]

However, it seems reasonable to pay some attention to the ratio between Omega-6s and Omega-3s. Although the impact on inflammation may be small, the cumulative effects over the course of decades may be significant.

Niacin (Nicotinic Acid) – Rivaling Omega-3s for Heart Health Support

Niacin, also known as Vitamin B3, is vital for good health. Niacin helps convert food into energy, build red blood cell counts, and synthesize hormones. Although your body manufactures niacin, you can also obtain it from foods.

At substantially higher levels — 1000-3000mg/day — niacin in the form of nicotinic acid significantly improves cholesterol levels. Nicotinic acid can lower LDL cholesterol by up to 15 percent, raise HDL cholesterol by as much as 35 percent, and lower triglyceride levels by 20-50 percent.[75] However, these high dosages should be taken under a physician's care, primarily because of concerns about potential liver complications.[ ] It is recommended that liver enzymes be monitored. Also, intense flushing, where the skins turns bright red, itches, and burns is associated with high levels of nicotinic acid. The flushing side effects can be reduced by pre-medicating with aspirin or ibuprofen prior to taking the niacin. Also taking niacin with a small snack high in fiber can delay absorption, reducing the intensity of flushing. Usually flushing is a startup consequence and will lessen as time goes on. People with diabetes or gout also need to be cautious about taking niacin as it can slightly raise blood glucose and uric acid.

Nonetheless, nicotinic acid supplements have been approved for sale by the Food and Drug Administration (FDA). Further, the intake of niacin at intermediate dosage levels — 100-1000mg/day — has been shown to improve the levels of both HDL and triglycerides. Coupled with other elements of nutrition, the intermediate dosage of niacin supplements may provide a meaningful contribution to long-term cardiovascular health.

The "411" on Niacin

Regardless of how much you take, niacin may have a role in advancing heart wellness. In one study, patients took 50mg of niacin in the form of nicotinic acid twice per day for three months. The patients on the niacin experienced an average 5 percent increase in "good" HDL.[76] As discussed in Chapter Two, even a small increase in HDLs can significantly lower the risk of heart attacks and strokes.

In another study, 500mg/day of niacin as nicotinic acid raised HDL by 10 percent along with lowering LDL by 5 percent and triglycerides by 5 percent. At 1000mg/day, improvements were even more dramatic, with an increase of 15 percent for HDL and a drop of 11 percent for triglycerides and 7 percent for LDL cholesterol.[77]

Choosing the right niacin supplements can be confusing. Three types of niacin are available -- nicotinic acid, niacinamide, and inositol hexanicotinate. Only nicotinic acid has been clinically shown to be effective for cholesterol management.

There are also three forms of nicotinic acid — immediate, sustained, and extended release. Even relatively low levels of immediate release nicotinic acid can cause an uncomfortable flushing side effect accompanied by an intense feeling of heat, tingling, and itching. Flushing can start a few minutes to a few hours after dosing and typically subsides within 30 minutes, often much sooner.

Higher dosage levels of nicotinic acid are available in a sustained release version. Although it reduces flushing, it has been associated with liver complications. The release mechanism never lets the liver recover during the day. The first two forms are available without prescription.

The third form of nicotinic acid, extended release niacin, is available as a prescription and has a lower incidence of liver complications than the sustained release version.

Depending on your unique conditions and health targets, niacin is a powerful nutrient that can play a role in your heart health agenda. Review your niacin intake. -- as well as all your supplement intake -- with your health care provider.

Red Yeast Rice: A Statin Alternative?

Red yeast rice can be found as a paste, whole dried grains, or as a ground powder. In these forms, it has been a common food in certain Asian diets.

Red yeast rice supplements can significantly lower total cholesterol and LDL ("bad") cholesterol. Red yeast rice, in fact, delivers a statin, the same active compound found in cholesterol-lowering medications. It is a natural source of lovastatin sold by Merck, one of the world's leading pharmaceutical companies.

For those preferring natural solutions, red yeast rice can be a legitimate option, but there are some risks and drawbacks if it's taken as a supplement. Back in 1999, when clinical studies were done on the efficacy of red yeast rice, supplement manufacturers could test and control for the statin-like compound. Today, however, since statins are prescription drugs manufactured by pharmaceutical companies, such testing and controlling is now prohibited, although red yeast rice supplements are still sold and widely available. One consumer report found significant differences in the levels of the active compounds across various manufacturers.[78]

Furthermore, red yeast rice supplements can cause the same side effects as any statin. According to the FDA, "Red yeast rice products are a threat to health because lovastatin can cause severe muscle problems leading to kidney impairment. This risk is greater in patients who take higher doses of lovastatin or who take lovastatin and other medicines that increase the risk of muscle adverse reactions. These medicines include the antidepressant nefazodone, certain antibiotics, drugs used to treat fungal infections and HIV infections, and other cholesterol-lowering medications."[79]

So rather than being an alternative to statins, red yeast rice should be considered as a naturally derived source for them. If you choose to use red yeast rice supplements, work with your healthcare professional to assess results and monitor any potential side effects.

CoQ10

Coenzyme Q10 (CoQ10), an antioxidant produced in the body, works in the muscle cells. Not surprisingly, CoQ10 is highly concentrated in the body's most active muscle, the heart. Studies have indicated that CoQ10 is useful for the treatment of congestive heart failure.[77] Unlike a heart attack – a sudden and severe instance of abnormal heart function -- congestive heart failure is caused by damage to the heart and occurs when the heart fails to pump enough blood to the rest of the body.

Like cholesterol, the liver manufactures CoQ10. While statin medications work to reduce the production of cholesterol, they also lower CoQ10 levels, possibly affecting heart health.[78,79]

Some people on statins do experience muscle pain and cramping, which may be the result of lowered CoQ10 levels. A smaller number have severe and painful muscle problems. Taking CoQ10 may help alleviate these symptoms; a study in which patients with statin-related symptoms took 100mg of CoQ10 revealed that pain intensity decreased by 40 percent. So for those taking statins, CoQ10 supplementation may offer an alternative to stopping treatment.[80]

Smaller amounts of CoQ10 can be found in foods; about

3-6mg per day are naturally ingested. Good food sources include certain kinds of fish (such as sardines), nuts, and olive and soy bean oils; these foods also offer a range of other heart health nutrients.

Your doctor may recommend CoQ10 if you are taking a statin medication—either the prescription version or as a red yeast rice. Some nutritional supplements blend red yeast rice and CoQ10.

Sodium Down and Potassium Up for Healthier Blood Pressure

Elevated sodium intake has long been a public health enemy. The medical community recognizes that high levels of sodium, found in salt, can raise blood pressure. For about a third of the population, small increases in salt intake can result in a large increase in blood pressure.   Among the more salt sensitive individuals, the effect of salt may be sufficient to create heart disease risks that require drugs. The impact of salt on blood pressure is modest for the rest of the population.   But even a small increase in blood pressure can accelerate the development of plaque in the arteries.

Sea Salt for Taste Not Nutrition

Many gourmet food stores offer a full range of salts from the world's oceans, seas, and salt lakes in beautiful, natural-looking packaging. The coarseness and ingredients of these salts provide a flavor dimension beyond that of normal table salt. Some gourmet chefs swear by the culinary advantages of certain types of salt.

Sea and table salt have the same basic nutritional value. Both mostly consist of two minerals: sodium and chloride. Some people look to sea salts for trace minerals, but as a rule, do not look to salt for healthy nutritional benefits.

You can get your minerals from a good variety of whole, healthy foods.

If it is taste, texture, or philosophy that you are after, sea salt can find a limited place in heart healthy cooking. However, taste benefits should not be confused with good nutrition and a "salt by any other name" is still salt.

Today most Americans get 2-3 times the amount of salt needed for healthy living. Salt can be found in the processed and prepared foods and snacks as well as takeout, eat-out, canned, and frozen foods. Figure 5.3 illustrates the major sources of salt intake for Americans.

Sources of Salt in the Standard American Diet

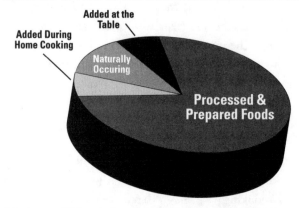

Figure 5.3. Sources of Salt in the Standard American Diet (From R.D. Mattes, et al *"Relative Contributions of Dietary Sodium Sources"* Journal of the American College of Nutrition, 10(4) (1991).

The danger associated with processed and prepared foods goes deeper. Not only does the American diet deliver excessive sodium compared to more natural, less processed diets, it also provides too little potassium. The traditional diet emphasizing fruit, vegetables, whole grains, and nuts offers more than twice as much potassium as the typical American diet.[83] Figures 5.4 and 5.5 break down the amount of sodium and potassium ingested, according to age and sex.

Sodium Intake

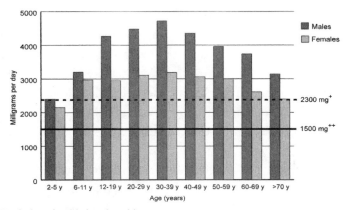

*Excludes salt added at the table.
+ Maximum Recommended
++ Target Recommended

Figure 5.4

Potassium Intake

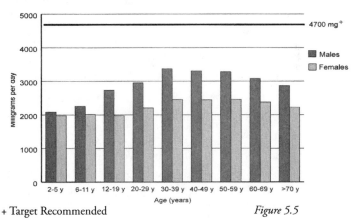

+ Target Recommended

Figure 5.5

Increased potassium levels alone have dramatically lowered salt sensitivity.[84] Studies have confirmed that higher levels of potassium can counteract the rise in blood pressure from a certain amount of sodium. Numerous studies have also found that when potassium intake declines, blood pressure and the risk of stroke rises.[86, 85] This is true across a wide range of heart and arterial risk factors including age, blood cholesterol level, obesity, fasting blood glucose level, and cigarette smoking and even among people with normal blood pressure who ingest less sodium. Overall, the combination of a low-sodium, high potassium intake is associated with both the lowest blood pressure levels and the frequency of stroke in individuals and populations.[87]

The National High Blood Pressure Education Program (NHBPEP) has identified both dietary sodium reductions and potassium increases as proven approaches to prevent and treat hypertension.[88]

The current recommendation targets a maximum sodium intake of 1.5 grams (1500mg).[89] This equals about 4 grams, or about 2/3 teaspoon, of table salt a day. For potassium, the current recommendation is 4.7 gram/day for all adults from food.[90] This level maintains lower blood pressure levels and reduces the adverse effects of sodium intake on blood pressure.

At present, dietary intake of potassium by all Americans is considerably lower. In recent surveys, the median intake of potassium by adults in the United States was approximately 2.8-3.3 grams/day for men and 2.2-2.4 grams for women.[ ]

The scientific evidence is strong. To maintain a healthy blood pressure and reduce the risk for stroke, it is important to consume target levels of potassium and achieve a balance between sodium and potassium in your diet. However, Americans consistently fail to obtain sufficient levels of potassium from their food. Overall, Americans only consume about half the targets set for healthy individuals. By contrast, they ingest at least two times the target level for sodium.

What About Salt Substitutes?

Salt substitutes help you lower your intake of sodium and increase potassium. Most table salt substitutes replace all or part of the sodium with some form of potassium. A single gram of salt substitutes can contain as much as 600 mg of potassium. A glass of orange juice provides 350 mg, a medium sized banana or a three ounce serving of tuna delivers 450 mg, a sweet potato or half-cup of white beans provides 600 mg.

However, some researchers believe that use of salt substitutes is less than ideal for human health.[ ] On one hand, salt substitutes support a taste for salt. At times, you may find yourself in search of this taste without the substitute being available, so you might indulge in traditional sodium chloride — table salt. Finding ways to change your eating patterns to lower your passion for salt is a better solution.

Additionally, not all sources of potassium provide the same nutritional benefit. The potassium found in salt substitutes is a potassium chloride. This is not the form of potassium typically found in whole foods. While most types of potassium can help with blood pressure regulation, the potassium found in foods have been shown to have broader health benefits.[ ]

Figure 5.6 ranks (page 102) food sources of potassium by milligrams of per standard amount, also showing calories in the standard amount. The recommend intake for adults is 4700 mg potassium.

Food, Standard Serving	Potassium (mg)[1]	Calories
Sweet potato, baked, 1 potato (146 g)	694	131
Tomato paste, 1/4 cup	664	54
Beet greens, cooked, 1/2 cup	655	19
Potato, baked, flesh, 1 potato (156 g)	610	145
White beans, canned, 1/2 cup	595	153
Yogurt, plain, nonfat, 8 oz container	579	127
Tomato puree, 1/2 cup	549	48
Clams, canned, 3 oz	534	126
Yogurt, plain, lowfat, 8 oz container	531	143
Prune juice, 3/4 cup	530	136
Carrot juice, 3/4 cup	517	71
Blackstrap molasses, 1 Tbsp	498	47
Halibut, cooked, 3 oz	490	119
Soybeans, green, cooked, 1/2 cup	485	127
Tuna, yellowfin, cooked, 3 oz	484	118
Lima beans, cooked, 1/2 cup	478	108
Winter squash, cooked, 1/2 cup	448	57
Soybeans, mature, cooked, 1/2 cup	443	149
Rockfish, Pacific, cooked, 3 oz	442	103
Cod, Pacific, cooked, 3 oz	439	89
Bananas, 1 medium	422	105
Spinach, cooked, 1/2 cup	419	21
Tomato juice, 3/4 cup	417	31
Tomato sauce, 1/2 cup	405	39
Peaches, dried, uncooked, 1/4 cup	398	96
Prunes, stewed, 1/2 cup	398	133
Milk, nonfat, 1 cup	382	83
Pork chop, center loin, cooked, 3 oz	382	197
Apricots, dried, uncooked, 1/4 cup	378	78
Rainbow trout, cooked, 3 oz	375	144
Pork loin, center rib (roasts), lean, roasted, 3 oz	371	190
Buttermilk, cultured, lowfat, 1 cup	370	98
Cantaloupe, 1/4 medium	368	47
1% milk, 1 cup	366	102
2% milk, 1 cup	366	122
Honeydew melon, 1/8 medium	365	58
Lentils, cooked, 1/2 cup	365	115
Plantains, cooked, 1/2 cup	358	90
Kidney beans, cooked, 1/2 cup	357	113
Orange juice, 3/4 cup	355	85
Split peas, cooked, 1/2 cup	355	116
Yogurt, plain, whole milk, 8 oz container	352	138

Figure 5.6 Selected Sources of Dietary Potassium

Cooling the Fires: Antioxidant and Anti-Inflammatory Nutrients

As discussed earlier, inflammation is a critical factor in the development of plaque. Antioxidants help keep inflammation in check.

The body naturally produces its own antioxidants. Researchers continue to explore what helps or harms the body's ability to produce these essential agents for healthy arteries.

Foods such as green teas, cocoa, blueberries, pomegranates, red wine, and a wide range of other fruits and vegetables also deliver antioxidants. Previously unknown fruits -- acai, mangostein and goji berries -- as well as traditional spices like cinnamon, clove, turmeric, oregano, and cumin are also powerful antioxidants.

Additionally, certain vitamins are antioxidizing, including Vitamins A, C, and E. Early clinical studies supported a theory that consumption of standard vitamin antioxidants could promote heart health.[91] Vast amounts of Vitamins A, C, and E were sold and consumed. However, later, more extensive studies failed to fully prove the vitamin antioxidant theory. The use of these vitamins fell out of favor with the mainstream medical community.

But strength of the antioxidant theory along with real data on the ability of antioxidants to cool the inflammatory process and promote arterial health has researchers looking deeper.[92] They have noted that many of the studies were conducted on individuals with known cardiovascular disease. Some researchers question whether sufficiently high dosages were used to assess the impact among a diseased population.[93] Other investigators wonder if antioxidant supplements would be more effective if used by younger people to slow plaque development and prevent the onset of cardiovascular disease.[94]

The truth is we are still exploring how antioxidants work within the body. Countless compounds have antioxidizing properties, yet just because a food or vitamin has antioxidizing ability outside the body does not mean that ability will hold true once ingested. Researchers continue to isolate and identify the most effective compounds.

Plums, for instance, have high levels of antioxidants when measured outside the body, but do not appear to raise the antioxidant levels in the bloodstream.[95] The researchers believe that the body does not easily absorb the antioxidant. In contrast, blueberries can deliver a noticeable climb in blood antioxidant capacity, but at least one-half cup of fresh berries is required to have a detectable impact. [96] Grapes and kiwifruit have been found to provide noticeable spikes in the blood levels of antioxidants. [97] However, researchers could not identify which compounds in the fruits were responsible for the increased levels. [98]

Researchers are now taking a more holistic approach and looking at the antioxidant capacity of an entire diet. [99,100] They have, for instance, found that multiple sources of antioxidants work together to reduce the levels of harmful LDL. [101]

Overall, we do know that diets high in vegetables, fruits, and whole grains – like the plant-based diets found in the heart healthy traditional societies – deliver many different antioxidants. Individuals following these eating styles also have lower levels of inflammation.

Rediscovering Vitamin D

The Vitamin D story represents one of the great nutritional tales about the relationship among modern lifestyles, longer lives, evolving science, and health policy.

Since the level of Vitamin D required to support life do not naturally occur in foods, the human body evolved to produce most of the Vitamin D it needed. Strong sunlight ignites the body's Vitamin D manufacturing process.

With urbanization came decreased exposure to the sun. During the late 19th and early 20th centuries, when cities were rapidly expanding due to industrialization, soot from burning wood and coal blocked the sunlight. As a result, people were unable to produce sufficient levels of Vitamin D and developed rickets, a softening of bones, particularly in children, that can lead to fractures and deformity. Cod liver oil, one of the few food sources of Vitamin D, became an early remedy.

In the 1920s, scientists isolated Vitamin D. It then could be manufactured and a wide number of foods, including hot dogs and beer, were fortified with Vitamin D. But in the late 1940s, the Federal government became concerned that too much was finding its way into the food supply and sharply restricted foods fortified with Vitamin D.

The government also established the recommended daily dietary intake of 400 IUs (international units) of Vitamin D. This is an amount that you can reasonably expect to consume in healthy diet that incorporates fattier fish or fortified cereals and milks, including soy milks. Ten minutes of summer sun with legs and arms exposed produce the equivalent of over 10,000 IUs.[102]

In subsequent decades, life spans expanded. An increasing number of cases of skin cancer resulted and were associated with excessive exposure to the sun. People now protect their skin by staying inside, covering up, and applying strong sunscreens.

Once again evidence suggests that Americans face a Vitamin D deficiency from all sources, both in what they eat and what their bodies make. Researchers are finding links between low Vitamin D and a host of diseases and health issues, including non-skin cancers , depression, and osteoporosis. [103,104,105]

Low Vitamin D levels have also been associated with heart health risks including high blood pressure, diabetes, and metabolic syndrome as well as increased incidences of strokes and congestive heart failure. [106]

Today Vitamin D levels are assessed though routine blood tests. Even the healthiest of diets may not deliver the levels of Vitamin D associated with advancing heart health. The amount of supplementation is dependent upon outdoor activity levels, gender, and age as well as geographical location. For example, people living in the northern part of the US will likely need more Vitamin D since the sun is weaker in those regions.

Vitamin D is available both as dietary supplements and prescription when high doses are needed. Vitamin D is also oil soluble and should be taken with fat, such as fish oil.

Supplements with 5000 IUs of Vitamin D also are readily available, more than 10 times stronger than the recommended 400 IUs. Remember though, Vitamin D can be stored in the fat in your bodies. Too much can be toxic. Again, work with your healthcare team with regard to this supplement.

Chapter 6
STRATEGIES FOR SMART AND DELICIOUS EATING

Those Living In The Mediterranean Are Not On A Diet – The Cooking Cardiologist.

Every year, the market is inundated with so-called new and revolutionary diets. Americans are receptive; most know that an appropriate weight is important for good health. We are even more aware that our waistlines and muscle tone define our attractiveness and sense of self. Shed the pounds and you also may no longer need cholesterol or blood pressure lowering medications.

The perils of obesity are well-documented. Doctors tell us to watch our weight and public health education efforts attempt to teach us ways to trim down. In schools and the workplace, the weight management message is reinforced. Extra weight can drive many into chronic conditions like diabetes, high blood pressure, and joint pain. It can lead to a deterioration of cholesterol levels, including increased LDL and decreased HDL levels. The extra weight costs us dearly in financial, emotional, and physical tolls.

The next time you are at the grocery store, waiting in line and watching your food travel down the big wide black conveyer belt, take a glance at the magazines. Three themes are repeated. Always a miracle weight loss program, usually a secret about someone and then there is always sex. Occasionally, editors combine all three into a single article. We are obsessed by all three, especially diets.

Yet with each passing year, Americans continue to get heavier, as Figures 6.1 and 6.2 show. In many parts of the United States, obesity doubled and even tripled over a 14-year period. These statistics illustrate that, despite our many efforts, the underlying factors fueling obesity have yet to be addressed.

Strong forces overwhelm the motivation to stay thin and popular diets are not working.

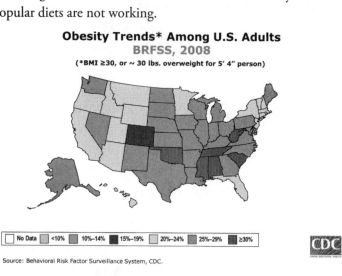

Figure 6.1 Obesity Trends Among Adults, 1994

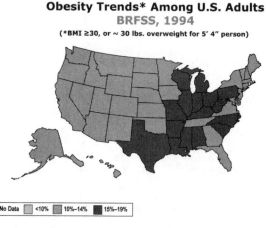

Figure 6.2 Obesity Trends Among Adults, 2008

The Obesity Blame Game

In *Mindless Eating*, researcher Brian Wansink wrote:

> We've all heard of somebody's cousin's sister who went on a huge diet before her high school reunion, lost tons of weight, kept if off, won the lottery, and lived happily ever after. Yet we also know about 95 times as many people who started a diet and gave up in discouragement, or who started a diet, lost weight, gained more weight, and give up in discouragement. After that, they started a different diet and repeated the same depriving, discouraging, demoralizing process. Indeed, it is estimated that over 95 percent of all people who lose weight on a diet gain it back again.[107]

Many factors are driving us to be a nation of overweight people. The problem starts with the complex set of government policies and programs that subsidize the delivery of calorie rich, nutrient-starved processed foods and meats. The Federal government spends billions of dollars each year to support the production of corn, soybeans, and wheat. These are the staple feeds for meat and dairy production and for the production of simple carbohydrates, sweeteners like high fructose corn syrup and white flour.

In the constant competition to drive down price, food manufacturers incorporate these low cost, nutrient-poor, calorie dense foods into an ever wider variety of foods.

Then there are the fast food restaurants. They learned that "super-sizing" pays handsomely in added profits. It takes the same service, equipment, and building to provide a child's portion as it does a supersized "value" meal. Yes, you get more, but more of the dollars find their way into profits than into costs of the additional food you receive.

Supersizing occurs outside of the fast food industry as well. Portion size in nearly all restaurants has steadily increased since the 1970s.[108] A typical restaurant meal has at least 60 percent more calories than the average meal made at home.[109] Ironically, only in the most elegant of eateries does the concept of "less is more" reign. Most chefs believe customers expect big platefuls of food when eating out.

Americans are eating more meals outside the home. Fewer households include a "stay-at-home" partner. For some, it is about economic necessity. All adults need to work to cover the financial demands of life. Others find personal fulfillment in a career. In this busy, fragmented society, family members often do their own thing with separate schedules and activities. Sitting down together for a home cooked meal is increasingly rare. Overall, America has less time to prepare the more wholesome, lower calorie, lower sodium meals that had been produced in our mother's kitchens.

The Caloric Balance Equation:

- Overweight and obesity result from an energy imbalance. This involves eating too many calories and not getting enough physical activity.
- Body weight is the result of genes, metabolism, behavior, environment, culture, and socioeconomic status.
- Behavior and environment play a large role in causing people to be overweight and obese. These are the greatest areas for prevention and treatment actions.

Adapted from U.S. Surgeon General's Call to Action to Prevent and Decrease Overweight and Obesity, 2001

At work and in daily activities, American burn fewer calories. Increasingly, Americans work in less physically demanding jobs. Even in the manufacturing sector, robots now perform the tasks once completed by calorie-burning humans. These changes have benefits. They have allowed for surges in productivity and improvement that in some cases has slowed the transfer of manufacturing jobs to lower wage economies. Unfortunately, they also alter the calorie balance. Fewer calories are now burned in the workplace.

The move from walkable neighborhoods to sprawling suburban developments has also lowered the number of calories burned. Car transport is required to nearly all activities outside the home -- schools, shopping, gym, and work. Unlike Europeans, American rarely walk to the local grocery store. More likely, we will drive to the store and wait five more minutes to pick a closer parking spot. Physical activity now falls exclusively into the domain of exercise, something to schedule. It is no longer an integrated part of daily life.

Weight gain among America's children is more than the result of junk food, overeating, and inactivity. It also is a function of the limits now placed on them. Dangers, we fear, lurk everywhere. Children cannot simply go out into the streets and play in our neighborhoods. Fewer kids are allowed to walk or bike to school anymore. Parents would rather see their offspring safe and confined as opposed to at risk and active.

Despite large scale, society-wide forces, we blame the individual for excessive weight. You are told that your weight is simply about caloric balance. Reduce the number of calories you consume and increase your physical activity and you will lose weight.

In the final analysis, though, individual restraint is being overwhelmed by other forces. The weight problem flows from a complex set of decisions and developments made over the course of the past generations. Much good has come out of these decisions. The caloric needs of hundreds of millions of people are met each day, in large quantities, and at low prices unimaginable a century ago. But progress has come with unanticipated costs — weight gain and the deteriorating healthful quality of foods.

In this context, excessive weight is as much a part of the sustainability debate as the use of fossil fuel. If we continue to add pounds to our population, we will face rising levels of chronic illness — and the continued and unsustainable escalation of health care costs.

Fueling the Burn

Many of the same factors driving weight gain in America also have led to a pattern of eating that directly assaults our arteries.

In a sense, it's like igniting a fire. Fire was one of humankind's first great discoveries. It provided heat for warmth, to cook, and to heat the kilns and forges that created the tools needed to build human civilization. Uncontrolled, though, fire reaps destruction. Every time you eat, you light up your system. Complex reactions, essential for health and life, take place.

Scientists and doctors use the term postprandial to define this excited post-meal period. Over a six-hour period after each meal, blood sugars, blood lipids, and inflammation levels rise. The human body has developed complex systems to regulate the post-meal, or postprandial, burn. Important nutrients like fibers, antioxidants, and healthier fats support the body's ability to keep the burn in control. Other nutrients, like simple carbohydrates and unhealthy or elevated levels of fats, can intensify the burn.

According to Dr. James O'Keefe of the Mid America Heart Institute, the "highly processed, calorie-dense, nutrient-depleted diet favored in the current American culture" frequently leads to exaggerated postprandial spikes in blood glucose and lipids. Dr. O'Keefe further writes that the eating patterns, "such as the traditional Mediterranean or Okinawan diets reduce the postprandial inflammation and thus cardiovascular risk. Improvements in diet exert profound and immediate favorable changes in these postprandial disturbances."[110]

With regard to blood pressure, the arteries will seek to relax, or dilate, after a meal. Blood pressure is then more likely to fall. This response may be part of our bodies' mechanism to control the postprandial impact. High fat diets, however, have been found to inhibit dilation. Over the course of a few weeks, or perhaps even days, the same highly processed foods high in sodium and low in potassium also cause blood pressure to rise.

As medical researchers seek to better understand the development of heart disease, the post-meal period is coming under increased study. They are finding that during an intense postprandial period, the inner layer of the arteries — the endothelium — becomes compromised. It is less able to send signals to regulate the arteries' ability to relax and produce compounds that can address inflammation. In this "hot" environment, LDL cholesterol can do major damage.

Researchers have also found that people with heart disease may have a more limited ability to control these post-meal spikes and that excessive spikes in blood sugars or fats in the blood after a meal can be better predictors of a cardiovascular event than at fasting levels.[111,112] Yet most people have their blood tested in the fasting state.

Of additional concern is that a large meal can be a trigger for heart attacks. In fact, the bigger the meal, the greater the risk.[113] Again, the challenge relates to the postprandial fire that burns following each meal. Supersizing is coming with considerable risk.

"Postprandial inflammation is an independent factor in evaluating food quality in addition to the well-known parameters of nutritional value, caloric content and amount of carbohydrates, fats, proteins, minerals and vitamins," writes Dr Andrew Margioris.[114] We need to eat not only with calories in mind and concern for nutritional balance, but also in ways that will help control the postprandial excitement in our arteries.

Say, for example, that you have been careful through most of the day, with oatmeal for breakfast, a salad for lunch, and a lowfat yogurt or healthy nutrition bar for a snack. You even found time to squeeze in a 30 minute walk or a 20 minute run. But it has been a hectic day. You now feel you have earned the right to splurge at dinner with an eight-ounce steak, a baked potato with a small amount of butter, a few spears of broccoli, and a piece of pie. You are probably aware that this meal is delivering too many bad fats, bad carbs, and too few healthful nutrients. It fails to provide the fibers, the minerals and the anti-inflammatory and antioxidant nutrients. A glass of red wine might help, but while some of the nutrients may be anti-inflammatory, alcohol is hardly a cure-all for nutritional imbalances. It can go from helpful to harmful after more than one glass.

While you ate healthfully throughout most of the day, this one meal set your system ablaze. The "fire" may only last for four to six hours, but some harm is done. That inner lining of the arterial wall -- the endothelium -- is faced with an inflammatory attack through which some cholesterol may have found its way into the arterial wall.

Now repeat this same process multiple times in a week, 52 weeks a year, over the course of decades. While you may have earned right to treat yourself, you are doing your arteries harm.

Matching Foods to Control the Burn

In modern America, we combine unhealthy ingredients into less healthy recipes. We then pair unhealthy recipes to create even unhealthier meals. The healthiest eating patterns utilize only the healthiest of ingredients to create healthy meals, for breakfast, lunch, dinner, and even snacks, allowing the body to control the postprandial effect.

Most Americans find it difficult to consume only the healthiest foods. But there is a healthy middle ground. In modern America, we must think about how we match — at each meal — the delicious foods that are good for us with those we love (but do not love us). At each meal, we need to assemble a more balanced collection of ingredients that support our bodies' natural ability to control the post-meal burn rather than igniting wild blaze. The power extends beyond simply creating a healthier balance. Good foods can somewhat blunt the impact of harmful ones.

The French Paradox

The traditional French diet, high in saturated fats from butter and cream, also has been associated with a reduced risk of cardiovascular disease when compared with an American-style diet.[115] This is known as the French Paradox.

The traditional French style of eating begins with unprocessed ingredients. Julia Child has said, "You don't have to cook fancy or complicated masterpieces, just good food with fresh ingredients."

But before jumping to Julia's *Mastering the Art of French Cooking* as a guidebook to heart health, note that while traditional French eating patterns may be somewhat healthier than the standard American diet, it is hardly heart healthy. In the Lyon Heart Study, people who had a heart attack were split into two groups. One group changed their diet, eating a Mediterranean style that included lower levels of saturated fats and higher monounsaturated fats. The other continued to enjoy a more traditional French cuisine. The group on the Mediterranean style diet had a 70 percent reduction in mortality over the one that maintained the traditional French diet![116]

Different ingredients work in different ways to support a healthier postprandial period. Fiber can slow the uptake of sugars into the blood stream. Soluble fiber and plant sterols can reduce the absorption of cholesterol. Relatively small intakes of Omega-3 can also help lessen the post-meal spikes in triglycerides.[117] Antioxidants found in spices, green tea, wine, cocoa, and a host of other ingredients that make good food great can cool the inflammatory effect of eating.

Smart eating is fundamentally about matching foods to assure that a sufficient amount of the good nutrients are always available to minimize the impact of those that are delicious but harmful. Smart eating also looks to curtail the oversized meal that can overwhelm the body's natural ability to control the post-meal fires.

A Lifestyle Approach to Heart Healthy Weight Loss

Many weight loss programs look to rapid weight loss. It may have taken you years, even decades, to add those extra pounds. Diets promise to return you to a lean body in weeks or months.

With many of these diets, there is restrictive "Phase One" in which you dive into the program with the clear objective of shedding weight quickly. As the pounds come off, you move to "Phase Two" which allows a wider range of foods. Ideally, you achieve a target weight during this phase. You then make your way to "Maintenance " -- an even more flexible "Phase Three" that provides you with a framework to maintain your weight. That, at least, is the theory.

If you are like most Americans, you will gain back the lost weight and then some. Only a very small minority of dieters remain successful.

Moreover, if the diet includes eating foods that come together to raise cholesterol, blood pressure, inflammation, and cause swings in your blood sugar levels, you are still doing yourself real harm -- even if you manage to keep off the weight.

Try a different approach. Instead of starting with the strictest of programs, take measured steps, one and then another, to change your eating patterns. Over time, you will find yourself healthier and lighter.

Think about it this way. When you are looking to improve your physical fitness, you do not start by running a marathon. You begin with a light workout, building toward more vigorous and rigorous training sessions. Getting in shape is a process. The same is true for healthy eating and weight management.

You also may never run a marathon. You may choose to walk enough each day simply to feel better, burn some calories, and improve your health. But working out a bit harder and longer each day offers additional health benefits.

Change your eating patterns in a similar way. Make the easier changes to what and how you eat. Build from there to achieve substantial gains in your heart health.

If you have the need or the motivation, you can elevate the intensity of your efforts. You can move to the most disciplined approaches to eating. Like a high performance runner or swimmer who works intensely to improve the few tenths of a second required to win the race, a very disciplined approach to eating will produce benefits. The additional improvement, though, will likely be small in comparison to the huge gains you made by moving from the riskiest of eating behaviors to a healthier balance between the foods that help and those that harm.

As you journey, you will move away from foods high in simple carbohydrates, sodium, and fats, particularly the unhealthier fats and towards foods that actively support heart and arterial health. These include high nutrient, high complex carbohydrate foods — fruits, vegetables and whole grains made more delicious by a mélange of spices and enjoyed with beverages that actively contribute to the healthy balance.

When pursuing these goals, take a longer term view. Unless you are facing a serious medical condition requiring quick dietary modifications, you can work toward sustainable changes. Step-by-step, your eating patterns will change over the course of months and years. You are looking to alter the cravings and eating habits that have been built over a lifetime. This takes time.

One pound of fat contains 3500 calories. In 15 years, 20 calories per day adds up to an additional 109,500 calories. Do the math — this equates over 30 pounds in additional weight. It may be around your waist, under your chin or on your buttock and thighs.

A few bites less, a few steps more each day, and you could have avoided or burned those 20 calories. Looking into the future, take the long-term view. Cut out a few more bites and exercise just a bit more, and in a few years, you will find yourself substantially thinner and healthier. Are you thinking that is too long? Consider this: if you are like Americans who binge diet, you will be heavier, not lighter, in a few years. Overall, the data indicates that dieters do not keep off the weight.

And here is perhaps another real benefit. Under sustained, slow weight *gain*, your arteries will be under constant attack. When slow, sustained weight *loss* and healthy eating come together, your blood chemistry will likely be far healthier -- in terms of blood sugar, blood fats, blood pressure and inflammation. You may still be overweight, but your arterial health will be improving. Slow but steady wins: you are the tortoise, not the hare, in this race.

Identify the Changes Most Important For Your Health

Before you start your journey, orient yourself. Have your blood pressure taken and blood chemistry assessed. Other risks factors -- family history of cardiovascular disease, weight, and level of physical activity should also be evaluated.

Along with informing you as to risks for heart disease, heart attack, or stroke, the doctor's examination will help define your key factors relating heart health, including cholesterol, blood pressure, blood sugar, inflammation, or some combination.

You then can develop goals and targets around the most important factors. If blood pressure is the pressing concern, then you can work towards lowering sodium intake and increasing potassium intake. Do you need to concentrate on cholesterol and other blood lipids? You can focus on minimizing harmful fats while seeking out certain soluble fibers, good fats, and plant sterols. If you need to better regulate your blood sugar, you can replace simple carbohydrates with higher fiber complex ones. If inflammatory markers like C-reactive protein (CRP) are concerning, look to fruits, vegetables, spices, and herbs that naturally deliver high levels of anti-inflammatory and anti-oxidizing nutrients.

Focusing on one or more risk factors is the starting point on your journey to heart healthy eating. In understanding your individual risks and personal eating preferences, you can assess whether changing eating patterns alone will be adequate and whether you will benefit from dietary supplements and medications.

As your journey toward healthier eating continues, you can broaden your focus and look beyond an immediate risk or condition. You can eat to optimize the overall health of your heart and arteries.

Improve Your Food Balance

While you have adopted the longer term view, you also now recognize that every meal, every eating event, counts.

How do you determine that right nutritional balance - the point where a meal contains enough of the healthier foods to adequately blunt the impact of the foods that may be delicious but harmful?

No single solution is right for everyone; answers lie in your unique risk profile. You may already know where to start — eat more vegetables, fruits, and whole grains cooked in healthful ways and cut down on highly processed, nutrient depleted foods. But eating healthy involves more than averaging the good with the bad through the course of the day; rather, it's about striking a balance during every meal and every snack.

Increasingly, properly prepared healthful foods should play a larger and larger role each time you eat. As you continue the journey, the healthful foods will come to dominate the plate; the harmful foods will play the supporting but delicious role.

Understand Your Eating Behavior

Next, look carefully into what and how you eat. Like most people, you have probably developed specific eating patterns.

Try keeping a food journal for a few weeks. By doing this, you'll likely find repetition of certain food choices and which meals and snacks are more out-of-balance than others and contain few if any heart healthy micronutrients. Generally, these involve foods with little or no fiber and are dominated by oils and fats, simple carbohydrates and salts.

By looking closely at breakfast, lunch, dinner, and snacks you can figure out what is (and what does not) meet your heart health needs. Some foods or ingredients may need to be cast away. Others may find their way onto your shelves. You may have to adapt your favorite recipes to include the more healthful ingredient. Or your favorite meal needs to be adjusted, with a particular dish being swapped out for a healthier one to attain a desirable balance. By tackling these smaller changes and making them part of the way you eat, you can move forward on your journey to healthier eating.

Sharing the Oversized Portions

Restaurants use the psychology of oversizing to maximize profits. They have discovered that they can charge you much more for bigger portion -- more than it actually costs them. They have learned that the perception of "value" of large sizes allows them to extract more dollars at each eating occasion. You can turn their profit motive to your advantage. If you are with family or friends, split everything you order – appetizer, main course and dessert. Perhaps you have may have to spring for an extra side salad (also check if the restaurant has a "sharing charge"). In splitting, you'll get your money's worth plus half the calories, a lot less salt, and still enjoy the full dining experience.

Or if you prefer your own meal, try doubling up on smaller appetizers, served in courses, and skipping the entree.

If the main meal is what you want, have the staff split the portion before it comes to the table. One-half comes on the plate, the other arrives with the check, packaged and ready to take home.

Consider Using a Nutrition Professional

A personal trainer keeps you on track with exercise. An annual physical or physician evaluation identifies emerging medical issues. A nutritionist or dietitian will help you evaluate how, what, and how much you eat as well as how to prepare foods and combinations best tailored to increase your heart health. They will also help you cope with eating out and other social occasions, avoiding temptations and boredom, as well as providing encouragement and suggestions as to developing and maintaining healthy eating habits.

Understand Why You Eat.

In counseling my patients as a registered dietitian, I speak from experience. Nearly 15 years ago, I lost 70 pounds and have kept it off. In my practice today, I use the same techniques that worked for me and many others.

I work on two levels with my patients. The first is the rational side of equation. It is about education, making sure people understand what they should and should not eat. We focus not simply on what will support weight loss but also what helps and harms heart health.

My patients also examine how they eat. Breakfast and snacks are important. Skipping meals and starving oneself is simply a bad way to try and lose weight and inevitably often leads to binging on unhealthy foods.

And of course we discuss how many calories can be eaten to achieve a target weight over a reasonable length of time.

To be successful, my patients and I also need to work on an emotional level. This is where we try to understand why they eat. In so many cases, they are eating not because they are hungry. Food is being used to cope with stress, anxiety, and sadness as well as boredom.

A big challenge is that emotional eating often has become habitual and a place in the everyday lifestyle patterns.

To break these habits, we start by understanding the difference between physical hunger and emotional eating. If you are physically hungry, you will feel it in your stomach—those rumbling, unpleasant stomach contractions (hunger pangs). You may also experience lightheadedness, difficulty concentrating, irritability or headaches. This usually starts four hours after a meal, and escalates after five hours. You will typically be open to any number of food options – good or bad -- to satisfy your hunger.

Emotional eating can come on suddenly and tends to be more specific. It is about craving a cookie, pizza, or burger. Emotional eaters tend to respond to certain triggers. You turn on the TV and haul out the chips. You go to the movies and eat popcorn. You fight with your spouse, you eat ice cream. Emotional eating can be a major roadblock on the journey to heart healthy eating and weight loss. For many of my clients, understanding the psychological factors that trigger emotional eating has been central to their success. - Susan Buckley, Registered Dietician

Track Your Progress

You'll need more than faith to track your progress. An annual physical is essential, not only to identify emerging health problems but also to provide actual data and trend. Through test results, tracked over time, you can tell whether cholesterol, weight, blood pressure, inflammation and blood glucose are in healthy or risky ranges. Start tracking in your twenties into your forties and then on to your sixties, eighties, and beyond. Information technology can help; many online applications, including Google Health, will let you obtain and organize your medical records online.

Tips from the Cooking Cardiologist
Rules to Eat By

- Put down your fork…give your palate a time to taste between bites, savor the flavor.
- Create interest in food…pride yourself in creating a home dish that fills you up without filling you out.
- Diet by deprivation does not work… have foods you always enjoyed but eat lesser amounts or change the recipe to reduce calories.
- Keep it simple. All you need is a 250 calorie deficit per day to lose 1/2 pound per week — or over 25 pounds per year. That equates to 125 fewer calores

eaten and 125 calories burned through increased physical activity.

- Beverages do count. Avoid diet drinks. They are like giving a reformed alcoholic a reminder each day to take a drink. They keep the sugar cravings going.
- Don't buy a diet books. Do it your way, slow and steady.
- Don't give up! Remember, if you are 100 pounds overweight, you have stored 350,000 calories in the bank. You can't withdraw that amount in one day.

SECTION III:
FROM TEXT TO TABLE

| Understand Your Risks | Understand the Power of Heart Healthy Nutrition | Create Your Heart Healthy Approach to Eating | Continue A Delicious Journey Toward Heart Health |

Chapter 7
TAKING SMART STEPS TOWARD A PLANT-BASED FOUNDATION

There is no love more sincere than the love of food
George Barnard Shaw (1856-1950)

Our eating decisions can go beyond taste preferences or health issues. For many, eating reflects personal philosophies.

Vegetarians enjoying mostly white breads, rice and pastas, cheese and butter, and highly salted or sweetened packaged foods still have an unhealthy diet. Their eating choices are rooted in a desire not to be the cause of an animal's death.

While not necessarily higher in nutrients, organic foods have other benefits. Produced without pesticides, herbicides, and growth hormones, these foods avoid the potential harm that may be cause by these chemicals. Organics also address broader environmental and sustainability goals.

The choice of sourcing foods locally may also have less to do with the nutritional value of fresh-from-the field. Instead, this choice may link to a desire to foster a more diverse local economy and a more integrated community.

The Plant-Based Foundation

Yet in discussions around vegetarian, organic, natural, and locally-sourced, there often is an implicit belief that they are intrinsically higher in helpful nutrients. Looking at these philosophies from a nutritional perspective, the key insight is this: These commitments and philosophies can help you move toward a plant-based diet with more nutrients that help rather than harm.

Processed and prepared food eating omnivores will need to give some additional thought about the role of meat, fish, eggs, and dairy in their diet.

Meat - A Supporting Role

There is no consensus that healthy plant-based eating eliminates all meats, fish, or dairy. Some heart healthy diets do exclude all animal-based products. Others support the inclusion of low fat dairy products and fish, and others still make room for modest levels of red meats and poultry.

As noted, even the heart healthy diets of traditional Mediterranean, rural China, or Okinawan societies included animal-based foods. Animal products, however, were not incorporated into every meal. They were used in celebrations and to add taste.

From a nutritional perspective, red meats pose a number of challenges. They contain saturated fats and are a source of dietary cholesterol. Certain meats, including beef, lamb, goat, deer, and bison are natural sources of trans fats. While the amounts of trans fats in these meats are low, the appropriate limit for trans fat also is very low. Processed meats are typically highly salted. Emerging evidence also suggests that meat consumption can fuel inflammation within your body.[118, 119]

All meats deliver significant amounts of protein, but as discussed earlier, there is no need to make protein the center of your diet. For an adult, 15-20 percent of your daily calories from protein is typically enough.

For any meal, limit meat intake to a single serving, typically defined as a four-ounce portion, about the size of a deck of cards.

But a four-ounce steak looks miniscule on a plate and certainly will not provide any sense of culinary wonder. A single serving in meat-and-potatoes meal is laughable; you likely will find yourself eating two, three, or even four helpings.

The picture changes dramatically if you cast aside the view that protein needs to take up center stage and consider meat as just another ingredient in delicious meals. The meats are used to enrich, but not rule, the foods on your plate.

The Kardea vegetable bourguignon with meat on page 175 is a healthier version of Julia Child's famous French dish. Looking for something for the barbeque? A Kefta Kabob serves a similar function. This Eastern Mediterranean version of the hamburger blends meat, spices, and in the Kardea Kitchen, ground beans.

Tips from the Cooking Cardiologist: Meat in a Plant-Based Diet

- At least one day per week should be 100 percent plant-based. Look for new recipes and eating-out options that can make this healthy choice enjoyable.
- With any meal, no more than one dish should have animal-based ingredients.
- Meat or dairy should always be in the minority in relation to fruits, vegetables, whole grains, and spices.

Spices: Cooling the Flames

Spices and herbs provide some of the most powerful anti-inflammatory, anti-oxidizing compounds available. While you may be in search of the latest "super fruit" for its antioxidant levels, there may be a much more powerful antioxidant sitting in your spice cabinet.

The heart healthy diets of traditional societies used spices extensively in meat preparation. This approach could be a heart healthy benefit of their eating patterns. Emerging evidence indicates that spicing — and marinating — meats can reduce the inflammation associated with meat consumption.[120]

Combining various spices also has shown a cumulative positive effect on blood lipids and arterial health, exhibiting their synergistic antioxidant activity.[121] Spice blends, in short, bring different compounds together to support heart health.

Use spices freely. When opening a fresh bottle of spices or herbs, pull off the shaker top and measure them in quarter, half, and full teaspoon amounts. Soon you will be combining a number of different spices and delivering a variety of antioxidant compounds that work in different ways within the body. These include Indian curries, North African and Middle Eastern sweet and savories, spice blends from Asia, and Latin fusions. And here is another important benefit--spice it up and you may need and crave less salt. Figure 7.1 illustrates the antioxidant capacity of herbs, spices, and cocoa.

Antioxidant Capacity of Herbs, Spice & Cocoa*

(*ORAC Measurement, Dried unless otherwise noted)	Common Usage Level	Antioxidant Level
Spice, Herbs & Cocoa/Chocolate		
Basil	1/2 teaspoon	1,689
Basil-Fresh	1 Tablespoon	481
Chili Powder	1/2 teaspoon	546
Cilantro-Fresh	1 Tablespoon	510
Cinnamon	1/2 teaspoon	6,688
Cloves	1/2 teaspoon	7,861
Cocoa Powder	1 teaspoon	4,250
Cumin	1/2 teaspoon	1,920
Curry	1/2 teaspoon	1,213
Garlic	1/2 teaspoon	168
Ginger	1/2 teaspoon	725
Marjoram	1/2 teaspoon	675
Mustard Seed	1/2 teaspoon	725
Oregano	1/2 teaspoon	5,000
Oregano-Fresh	1 teaspoon	700
Paprika	1/2 teaspoon	450
Parsley	1/2 teaspoon	1,850
Pepper-Black	1/2 teaspoon	688
Peppermint-Fresh	1 teaspoon	700
Tarragon Fresh	1 teaspoon	777
Thyme-Fresh	1/2 teaspoon	688
Turmeric	1/2 teaspoon	3,975

Source: Compiled from United States Department of Agriculture Report "Oxygen Radical Absorbance Capacity of Selected Foods" November 2007; Adapted by Kardea to more common usage rates.

Figure 7.1 Antioxident capacity of herbs, spices and cocoa.

Fish – Finding the Sustainable, Healthy Balance

The traditional diets of the Eskimos and Inuits have been associated with a low risk of heart disease. Very high in fish, these diets deliver as much as 14 grams per day of Omega-3 fatty acids. In the United States, the average intake of these types of Omega-3s is about .2 grams per day.

Clinical research continues to support increasing the levels of Omega-3s typically found in fatty fish like salmon, sardines, tuna, and mackerel. Shellfish also can be a good source of these healthy fatty acids.

Few people eat as much fish as the Inuits did, not even the Inuits today. For one thing, the world fish stock is fast becoming depleted. And depending upon what part of the country you live in, fish can be quite expensive and not as readily available or fresh. Plus, oceans have been polluted, and fish consumption can carry high levels of heavy metals and other chemicals that can do harm over time and if eaten in sufficient quantities. Figure 7.2 illustrates the mercury levels of various types of fish.

Mercury Levels & Sustainability		
LEAST MERCURY	**MODERATE MERCURY**	**HIGH MERCURY**
Enjoy these fish:	Six servings or less per month:	Three servings or less per month:
Anchovies	Bass (Striped, Black)	Bluefish
Butterfish	Carp	Grouper*
Catfish	Cod (Alaskan) *	Mackerel (Spanish, Gulf)
Clam	Croaker (White Pacific)	Sea Bass (Chilean)*
Crab (Domestic)	Halibut (Atlantic)*	Tuna (Canned Albacore)
Crawfish/Crayfish	Halibut (Pacific)	Tuna (Yellowfin)
Croaker (Atlantic)	Jacksmelt	
Flounder*	(Silverslde)	
Haddock (Atlantic)*	Lobster	
Hake	Mahi Mahi	
Herring	Monkfish*	
Mackerel	Perch	
(N. Atlantic, Chub)	(Freshwater)	
Mullet	Sablefish	
Oyster	Skate*	
Perch (Ocean)	Snapper*	
Plaice	Tuna (Canned chunk light)	
Pollock	Tuna (skipjack)*	
Salmon (Canned)**	Weakfish (Sea Trout)	

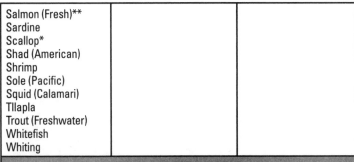

Salmon (Fresh)** Sardine Scallop* Shad (American) Shrimp Sole (Pacific) Squid (Calamari) Tilapia Trout (Freshwater) Whitefish Whiting		

*Fish in Trouble! These fish are perilously low in numbers or are caught using environmentally destructive methods. To learn more, see the Monterey Bay Aquarium and the Blue Ocean Institute website, both of which provide to fish to enjoy or avoid on the basis of environmental factors. ** Farmed Salmon may contain PCB's, chemicals wHh serious long-term health effects.

Figure 7.2 Mercury Levels of Fish

Some fish contain higher levels of these pollutants than others. Tuna and swordfish have more heavy metals concentrated in their fats. Wild salmon have somewhat less and sardines even less. Farm raised salmon may have fewer heavy metals but may contain higher levels of PCBs, a chemical banned in the 1970s but still found in the sediment of oceans, lakes, and rivers.

Wild Versus Farm Raised

Many prefer wild salmon over their farm raised cousins. In part, some people prefer the taste of the wild salmon. Others find fault in fish farming methods. Current methods pollute surrounding waters. In terms of the health profile, the research is mixed. The levels of Omega-3s, for instance, differ significantly with the type of salmon. The Atlantic salmon, the primary species used in fish farming, contain high levels. Some species of wild salmon may contain more, others less.

As we look at improving the eating habits of billions of people around the world, fish farming will have a place and fish farmers are developing more ecologically friendly methods. Sustainably grown fish from the farm will be sold alongside organic fruits and vegetables, grass-fed beef and free-range chicken.

Fish in the Everyday Diet

Cholesterol is only found in the animal-based foods, not plants. Fish and shellfish are no exception (see Figure 7.3). With the National Institutes of Health recommending consuming less than 300 mg of cholesterol per day, a single serving of high Omega-3 sardines can deliver about half your daily allotment of dietary cholesterol. The same amount of shrimp, another moderately good source of Omega-3s, delivers two-thirds.

In developing your smart and delicious style of eating, think about seafood in much the same way as meat. It should play an enriching, supporting role and not the lead. Enjoy seafood with lots of plant-based ingredients. A tuna salad should be just that – a mix of lots of vegetables that includes some tuna and some dressing. Try our Mediterranean tuna or sardine salad on page 204.

Used smart, seafood is both healthy and delicious. Take the Kardea barley paella for example. The leading ingredients in this meal are a cholesterol-lowering, fiber rich whole grain, and vegetables. Seafood can deliver a daily target for Omega-3s. Some highly spiced chicken chorizo sausages can define the flavor difference between a bland knock-off of a great Spanish recipe and something truly delicious. The Cooking Cardiologist recipe for Green Tea Poached Halibut with Blueberry Salsa also delivers a solid antioxidant punch and a wonderful sauce that brings delight to the surrounding dishes.

Omega-3 and Cholesterol in Selected Seafood		
Type	Omega-3s (mg/4oz)	Cholesterol (mg/4oz)
Anchovies	1477	97
Catfish		
Channel, farmed	206	73
Channel, wild	246	82
Cod	221	63
Eel	215	144
Flounder	227	55
Grouper	285	42

Haddock	262	84
Halibut	530	47
Herring, Atlantic	1162	81
Mackerel, Atlantic	1373	86
Pompano	830	73
Salmon		
Atlantic, farmed	2448	72
Atlantic, wild	2098	81
Chinook	1982	97
Coho	1458	72
Pink-Canned	1199	93
Sockeye	1402	99
Smoked (Lox)	513	26
Sardines	1119	162
Sole	227	55
Striped Bass	1102	117
Snapper	366	54
Swordfish	934	57
Trout		
Rainbow, farmed	1316	66
Rainbow, wild	988	79
Tuna		
Albacore, canned in water	971	51
Bluefin	1713	56
Light, canned in water	308	23
Yellow Tail	249	51
Clams		
Canned	324	76
Steamed	324	76
Crab		
Alaskan King	544	81
Blue	540	114
Dungeness	449	87
Crayfish	185	156
Lobster-Maine	96	82
Lobster-Spiny	514	103
Mussels	891	64
Oysters		
Pacific Steamed	1569	114

Pacific Raw	784	57
Eastern Steamed	1280	120
Eastern Raw	441	29
Scallops	416	60
Shrimp	314	222

USDA Nutrient Data Laboratory Database, Release 21 (2008)

Figure 7.3 Omega-3s and Cholesterol in Fish

Canned fish

For many Americans, eating fish is defined as a canned white albacore tuna swimming in mayonnaise. While tasty, it is not the best way to get Omega-3s.

While typically higher in Omega-3s than the canned light tuna, the albacore tuna are higher in mercury. The stocks of albacore tuna are dwindling.

Consider bringing smaller canned fish, like sardines, into your diet. These smaller fish are sustainable, grow quickly, and have less chance of containing high levels of mercury and can offer higher levels of Omega-3s than even the albacore tunas.

What About Dairy?

The original food pyramid was developed by the National Dairy Council and called for milk with every meal. The human, in fact, is the only animal species when weaned returns to drinking the "milks of mothers" of another species.

Many people of Mediterranean, African, or Asian descent are lactose intolerant and lack an enzyme that enables the digestion of dairy proteins. Ingestion of dairy products results in bloating and cramping.

Cream and butter are high in saturated fat and not heart healthy. Ghee, a clarified butter common in India, consists of pure butter fat, so while red meat makes up a relatively small portion of the Indian diet, the incidence of heart disease is very high.

In the 1960s and 70s, the Finnish had a diet very rich in dairy products, cheeses, and butter. The incidence of heart disease was the highest in the world. The country took note and made major changes in fat consumption. The result: A very significant drop in heart disease.

Adapting your love of dairy products offers an excellent example of the journey to heart healthier eating. The Cooking Cardiologist recommends reducing the amount of fat in the milk you drink. If you enjoy whole milk, then try 2 percent, then 1 percent, then to skim milk. Do it gradually. Soon your tastes will alter and when this happens, if you return to whole milk, you will think you are drinking cream. Consider "milks" made from soy, rice, oats, or almond. Lactose-free substitutes are also now widely available, but lactose-free whole milk is just as heart-harmful as regular whole milk and should be avoided.

Cheese: The Glory, the Vice

You may think that the delicious cheeses of France and Italy are as much about the Mediterranean diet as red wine, fresh vegetables, and olive oil. Not true. The healthy Mediterranean diet uses cheese sparingly, to add sensory delight. In the Lyon Heart Study discussed in Chapter Six, French patients with heart disease who switched to a healthier Mediterranean diet with lower saturated fats from dairy and higher in fruits, vegetables, and plant-based oils experienced a far lower level of a heart "events" than those remaining on the traditional French diet. Nonetheless, cheese making is a fine art and cheese makers through the ages have created some extraordinary taste sensations.

Cheese Tips From the Cooking Cardiologist

- Never start entertaining with cheese and crackers. If you set out the cheese before the meal, when everyone is hungriest, lots will be eaten. Instead use bean spreads like hummus or a spread made from white beans. A few appetizing vegetables like fresh roasted pepper, olive tapenades, or chunks of artichoke hearts settle nicely on a cracker, as will a sardine salad or Mediterranean tuna salad.

- Great cheeses should be enjoyed at the end of the meal, with some fruit and nuts. After the meal, with hunger satisfied, a small chunk can still delight the senses.

- Enjoy a mozzarella-free pizza. Add a touch of parmesan cheese to garlic, basil, and any grilled vegetable to satisfy a pizza craving.

- Never use macaroni with cheese or fettuccine Alfredo as the centerpiece of the meal. At the very most, a small portion can be added alongside a much larger portion of cooked vegetable and salad. And look to move the cheese and simple carbohydrate recipe out of your eating routines. These should be reserved only for special occasions.

Carbohydrates Get Complex

Simple carbohydrates -- foods created from white flours, white rice, and other foods with easily digested starches or lots of sugars -- can do our bodies real harm. But certain simple carbohydrates also deliver important nutrients. Potatoes, for instance, are an excellent source of potassium. Other starchy vegetables -- sweet potatoes, carrots, parsnips, and yams — provide a variety of nutrients, including high levels of naturally occurring Vitamin A compounds. Sweet potatoes were even a staple in the traditional Okinawan diet.

An important element of smart and delicious eating lies not with the complete exclusion of the simple carbohydrates. While whole grains are nutritionally better, trying pairing the simple carbohydrate with something that will make it more complex, thus slowing the rapid release of sugar into the blood stream. Good "matches" include foods high in complex carbohydrates and fibers, good fats, and proteins. As with meat, simple carbohydrates can enrich the eating experience, rather than ruling the plate and dominating the meal. For example, a heaping bowl of pasta with sauce becomes pasta Fagioli, a comfort food in many Italian households comprised of equal amounts of pasta, beans and vegetables, the recipe for which is on page 180.

Another example is red beans and rice. The rice does not need to be whole grain as the beans pick up the fiber. Many dishes can be switched to different complex carbohydrates such as couscous to quinoa, or a corn tortilla instead of a flour tortilla.

Fruits are another example. An apple contains simple carbohydrates, but leaving the peel on increases the fiber content.

Surprisingly, some of the best sources of complex carbohydrates are green vegetables! Along with lettuce, broccoli, green beans, and cucumbers, spinach is largely carbohydrates, with two-thirds coming from fiber. So in addition to providing vitamins, minerals, and other micronutrients, greens help establish a well-matched balance of foods to support postprandial control.

At the other end of the spectrum are desserts which, while delicious and delightful, can often deliver harmful simple carbohydrates, excessive sugar, bad fats, and few helpful nutrients. Desserts should be used to enrich the eating experience, rather define it. Use them sparingly, to end the meal with a taste treat, not as another course. Dessert should be a delight designed to extend the time with family and friends during a meal.

For the Love of Bread

My culinary coming of age evolved as artisanal breads burst on to the cooking scene. Crusty French, Italian, and sourdough breads of all shapes, sizes, and tastes; semolina breads with sesame coatings; rosemary olive boule; and pure white crusty baguettes continue to be favorites.

It was not just that I loved these breads. They often defined how I thought of a good meal. It might begin with a slice or two dipped in good extra-virgin olive oil. The crust of bread was the tool with which I pushed a salad onto my fork. The main meal would not end until the last of the sauce was cleaned from my plate with a piece of bread.

It was not just that I loved bread. It was that bread had become central to the way I ate. It was part of my eating lifestyle.

It took time for me to understand that a great meal need not be accompanied by bread. It required that I change how I ate and how I thought about how a meal starts, comes together, and ends.

Once I recognized this relationship, I found that I could redefine my thoughts about a meal. Not only did I eat less bread, I ate less. Bread was my way of eating beyond where I was satisfied. It was my way of eating till my plate was clean -- sometimes well beyond being full.

In looking to make changes, think carefully about what defines a meal for you. Sometimes you can modify how you see certain types of food and with that, your ability to control how much you eat becomes easier.

— Rob Leighton

Processed vs. Whole Grains

We look back at many of the heart healthy traditional diets and think "whole grain." In fact, many of the recipes of these cuisines use processed grains. The white rice used in Spain, China, and Japan, the breads of France, the pastas and risottos of Italy, the pitas of the Eastern Mediterranean, and the couscous of North Africa all are processed grains.

Beyond the fact that the processed grains may enhance the flavors and textures of these dishes, a more fundamental reason for the processing of grains probably exists. In traditional societies where poverty was widespread, adequate daily caloric intake was far from certain and cooking required much time utilizing scarce fuels, processing the grains afforded important benefits. Along with the more complete and more rapid absorption of the available energy, they could be cooked more quickly, saving time and fuel.

Today, however, thanks to modern cooking and preparation methods, traditional recipes using processed grains can be replaced with whole or higher-fiber alternatives. Steamers, rice cookers, and crock pots make whole grain cooking easy and convenient.

Expand the Breakfast Repertoire

You have fasted overnight and your system has had a chance to quiet down; blood sugars, triglycerides, and inflammatory levels should be at their most controlled levels. At this point, you can breakfast in a way the starts the controlled burn needed to energize you. Or you can set your system ablaze -- triggering the cascade of reactions that do arteries harm.

The good news is that breakfast can easily be made into a heart healthy meal. Along with fruit, whole grains and high fiber can be enjoyed in the form of oatmeal and bran cereals. Coffee, tea, and cocoa can deliver useful antioxidants as would cinnamon on your cereal. A teaspoon of natural nut butter can replace the nutrient poor butter, margarine, or creamed cheese spread on bread.

If you are in a hurry, try a handful of almonds or walnuts. High in many of the heart healthy micronutrients, they include a good combination of complex carbohydrates, healthy fats, and proteins that can sustain you through the morning hours.

Or you can enjoy a healthy nutrition bar or a smoothie. These can be good on-the-go solutions, but rather than focusing high protein, look for a good nutritional balance that also delivers the complex carbohydrates and good levels of other healthful nutrients.

A range of other foods can be incorporated into a breakfast repertoire. In the Eastern Mediterranean, many start the day with hummus, a chickpea-sesame spread. Throughout South and Central America, red or black beans are a breakfast staple. These beans deliver similar levels cholesterol-blocking soluble fiber found in oatmeal. In Asia, vegetables are commonly incorporated into the morning meal. Smoked, baked, and pickled fish are found on breakfast plates in North and Eastern Europe, delivering healthy fats including Omega-3s and good quality proteins.

Mixing It Up with Eggs and Other Foods

How many eggs can you eat in a heart healthy week of eating? An average American egg contains 200-250 mg of cholesterol. Current guidelines recommend no more than 300 mg per day. Less is better, the 300mg per day is the limit, not the goal. Two eggs will put you beyond your daily intake of cholesterol. Then eat any fish, meat, cheese or poultry, and you will be pushing well beyond the limit.

Yet for many, eggs for breakfast are as American as apple pie is for dessert. A heart healthy diet can incorporate some eggs, but let's start with understanding how to you use them.

Start by thinking about eggs the same way you think about meats. Use them to make other healthy foods more delicious. Again, a real problem with eggs often lies with how they are matched with other foods. Fried in butter and served with bacon, cheese and home fries, you have created a meal way out of balance. Enjoying a single egg, poached or boiled, with a bowl of oatmeal and a piece of fruit provide a smart balance. You removed the unhealthy fats, salt and simple carbohydrates. You have added soluble fibers that can reduce of the amount cholesterol that will be absorbed into the blood. The plant-based nutrients and minerals like potassium can help fight inflammation and support healthy blood pressure.

Also recognize that pure dietary cholesterol will not significantly raise levels of cholesterol unless coupled with saturated fat intake. The egg yolk contains both. The white part (albumin) is fat and cholesterol free. In the Cooking Cardiologist's opinion: "don't let the egg industry insist that you eat the yolk." Try cooking with only the egg white or use only one yolk per serving. If you crave a breakfast sandwich, skip the cheese and ham. Fry one egg or two egg whites in olive oil over a low heat. Serve on a whole grain roll with a bit of thyme, a slice of tomato and a lettuce leaf.

There is some good news on the horizon. In Singapore, eggs from carefully bred chicken on a controlled diet have been reported to contain only 70-80 mg of cholesterol.

Snacking: Getting It Right

Snacking can be particularly challenging. We often think of the snack as the best time for an indulgence. Unfortunately, it may be the worst. Snacks offer fewer opportunities to find a healthful food balance. Alone, a bag of high sodium, simple carbohydrate potato chips, baked, kettle-fried, or spiced, can spark the unhealthy fires. So can salted pretzels. Even a sugar-free cookie baked with white flour and lots of oil is no better.

As a rule, enjoy your indulgences at mealtime, matched with healthful foods. The snack is a bridge to the next delicious, balanced meal. Keep snacking as healthy as you can. Raw vegetables alone or in a small salad make a great snack. A small lower-sugar smoothie or nutrition bar with fiber, protein, and fruit are great. A handful of nuts with some dried fruit can work. Try a bean spread like a hummus.

But What About My Chocolate Craving?

Let's face it: Some of us must have our chocolate, no matter what. So here are some guidelines.

- The darker the chocolate, the more heart healthy compounds it contains.
- Look for natural as opposed to alkalized (Dutch) chocolate. Alkalizing creates a milder tasting chocolate but has been shown to reduce the levels of the heart healthy compounds
- Keep your intake to 1 to 1.5 ounces of chocolate, remembering that one of the great luxuries of chocolate is not just the taste. The wonders of chocolate also come from the way it melts in your mouth. Savor your chocolate, eating it slowly and with concentration. You are likely to discover the marvelous flavor subtleties.

Beverages: Your Source for Added Antioxidants!

When looking at the oversizing of America, consider how we are using drinks. Beverages deliver large amounts of the simple sweeteners with lots of calories that can lead to an intensified post-meal spike in blood sugar. If you consume cream in your coffees, chais, or lattes, you are also adding saturated fats that can quickly interfere with your arteries' performance. And while diet beverages don't provide the calories, sugars, and fats that hurt, they also fail to deliver helpful nutrients.

The weight you may have gained over the years may have come from beverage calories added each and every day. Sharply reducing the calories from what you drink is a simple way to start controlling your weight.

Yet beverages can help promote heart health. In addition to wine, a Mediterranean meal may finish with spiced teas or small servings of dark coffees. These beverages provide antioxidants and other plant-based compounds to traditional heart healthy diets.

Besides water, traditional Asian diets included teas, providing nutrients that improve arterial health. One study, however, found that tea works best when paired with foods. Probably because of its caffeine levels, tea can increase blood pressure when consumed alone. When taken with a meal, however, this short-term impact on blood pressure is eliminated.[122]

Fruit juices are not fruit. You can eat a half grapefruit or a whole orange at breakfast, each delivering not only the juice but also ample amount of fiber. A piece of fruit is a naturally balanced food. It takes 3-4 oranges to make that one eight ounce glass of orange juice, delivering lots of calories and sugar. Alone, the juice is no longer a balanced food. The upside is that fruit juices can be good sources of vitamins, minerals, and other nutrients. So, again, if it is juice in the morning you love, think about it as yet another indulgence. Enjoy it, but limit the amount you consume. Buy yourself some small juice glasses and enjoy it during a well-balanced meal.

Researchers originally looked to the French consumption of red wine -- typically with meals, often at lunch and dinner – as being heart healthy. Red wine delivers a significant number of micronutrients associated with improvements in cardiovascular health. A glass or two per day of alcohol has proven to be anti-inflammatory.

Beyond the antioxidants found in wine, alcohol – in moderation -- has been shown to be heart healthy. A study released by the Harvard Medical School and the Harvard School of Public Health found that liquors and beer deliver some of the same health benefits as wine.[123] The study focused on the relationship between moderate alcohol intake and a reduction in inflammation.

The Harvard study compared levels of C-reactive protein (CRP), a measure of inflammation in the blood used to assess risks of cardiovascular disease, and alcohol consumption of almost 12,000 women. Some drank beer; others, wine; and still others, liquors. Another group enjoyed some of each. Overall, the association between alcohol and inflammation levels was found to be related to level of alcohol consumption rather than type of alcohol consumed. Researchers discovered that one drink per day for women and up to two for men helped lower inflammation. More than that actually promoted inflammation.

The Role of Natural and Organic

For many, "natural" and "organic" connotes healthy. Overall, eating organic and natural will help move you towards a healthier style of eating. You are likely to consume fewer highly processed foods that are rich in calories and salt and low in helpful nutrients. You are likely to eat more whole foods.

Whether natural, organic or artificial, a food can be equally as harmful. All-natural potato chips or ice cream deliver the same nutrients that harm with few of the nutrients that help. They may be delicious, but they may be as harmful as their artificially flavored counterparts.

Organic fruits and vegetables may not have any intrinsic nutritional advantages over standard produce.[124, 125] Soil, sun, species and season are the more critical variables in determining nutrient levels. The type of soils and the weather alter the nutrient content of the crops. The genetic profile of one kind of fruit or vegetable may deliver higher nutrient value than another. When the crop is harvested also has an effect on the nutrient value.

Natural and organic meats, however, may have a nutritional advantage. They may be leaner. The type of fat also may be different with grass-fed and free range meats delivering lower levels of unhealthier fats and higher levels of the healthier fats. They also are produced without growth hormones or antibiotics.

Keeping It Natural with Cookware

Commercial kitchens and professional chefs rarely use non-stick pans as they use high heat to sear foods and abuse the pans on a daily basis. The chef also does not have to clean the pan. Restaurants have industrial type pot scrubbing equipment for that job. For your own home, you are the pan scrubber so non-stick pans are worth the investment, but take care to purchase the right ones.

When you hear "non-stick," you may think "Teflon." This is the trademarked name for polytetrafluoroethylene (PTFE). High heat can soften the compound and even release it into the air. The airborne compound can be toxic to birds, especially household canaries. The surface can flake, bubble, and peel. If your non-stick pan has scratch marks, time to toss it.

The manufacture of Teflon also impacts the environment. A chemical used to make Teflon, PFOA (perflouorooctanoic acid), has been found in humans. While not in the pan itself, it has entered our environment and can be toxic. In a study of over 12,000 children in West

Virginia, PFOA was linked to higher cholesterol readings in children with higher PFOA in their blood.

Select pans that are Teflon free and that use a ceramic or anodized coating. Not only do they make cooking easier but they are green friendly.

Is Fresh from the Field Better?

Many people believe that fresh from the field is healthier and vine-ripened foods do taste better. Most who have eaten fresh-picked tomatoes agree that their store-bought counterparts are far less delicious. And in general, as produce ages, it loses its flavor. Fruits and vegetables shipped from a distant place also may have been picked before they are fully ripe. While this practice helps prevent spoilage in transport, how does it affect the nutritional content? Consider the following:

- Blackberries and strawberries had the highest antioxidant values during the green stages, whereas red raspberries had the highest levels when mature.[126]
- For blueberries, antioxidant levels were maintained during the first three weeks in storage, and for some varieties, increased during cold storage.[127]
- Tomatoes harvested at full ripeness exhibited the highest level of Vitamin A compounds and antioxidant activity. On the other hand, no significant differences in Vitamin C content were observed at different ripening stages, whereas the antioxidant activity showed slight but significant decreases as the tomato moved to an overripe stage.[128]
- For sweet peppers, the immature green peppers showed the highest content of micronutrient polyphenol. The red ripe fruits had the highest content of Vitamins A and C.[129]
- For apples, long-term storage, both at refrigerated

temperature and under controlled atmosphere conditions, had no influence on the antioxidant activity. [130]

- With lettuce, some compounds were lost during storage, while others increased. [131, 132]

Belgian scientists reported that fruits and vegetables maintained their antioxidant content in the days after purchase, even as telltale signs of spoilage appeared. In some cases, antioxidant levels actually rose. Three types of micronutrients measured -- phenolics, ascorbic acid, and flavonols, a trio of chemical classes associated with antioxidant content -- remained stable throughout the study. The levels of one of these compounds, the phenolics, actually increased.[133]

Your decision to buy fresh and local thus may have less to do with nutritional value than personal philosophy and preference. Farm fresh foods can taste better. The agricultural methods may be more sustainable and the carbon footprint lower. It also can support more diverse local economies. But the simple fact is that eating more vegetables and fruits, whether from the local farm stand or distant shores, supports a healthy heart.

Health Benefits of Being a "Seasonal Eater"

The nutritional values of any fruit or vegetable are created, in part, by the amount of sun, the minerals in the soil, and the length of the growing season. Your local environment thus may or may not create healthier foods than those imported from distant places.

A commitment to eating seasonally, however, has very real health benefits and can help you move toward a plant-based foundation diet.

As the different crops arrive throughout the year, seasonal eaters break out of their cooking and eating patterns. They try new vegetables and new ways of cooking them. With abundant fruit crops, the seasonal eater uses them for more than a snack, a dessert, or a topping on the morning cereal. Fruits find their way into gazpachos and other soups, salsas, and salads.

There are lots of ways to going seasonal (and local). Try purchasing a "share" of the harvest of an area farm. Each week, the farm will deliver a collection of that week's crops to your door It is up to you to figure out what do with all the chard and strawberries that arrive early in the season; the summer squash, green beans, and peaches that come next; and the tomatoes, eggplant, apples, and butternut squash that follow. Along the way, you also will be provided with bunches of herbs, like parsley, mint, basil, and rosemary.

The internet has names of local farmers who sell produce as well as the schedule of nearby farmers' markets. Your commitment to eating locally and seasonally will help expand your repertoire of delicious plant-based recipes.

Chapter 8

TECHNIQUES FOR HEART HEALTHY COOKING

I was 32 when I started cooking; up until then, I just ate."
Julia Child

*What distinguishes a fabulous executive chef from a great cook
is only one degree."*
The Cooking Cardiologist

Cooking distinguishes humanity. No other living creature cooks. Food preparation utilizing heat has allowed humankind to develop from a primitive existence to fuller, more enriching lifestyles. Cooked food offers immense sensory pleasure and tastes delicious.

The offering of a wonderful meal, cooked with one's own hands, can convey love and caring. Cooking offers the opportunity for creative self-expression. Kitchenware provides the tools of the artistry and the plate is the canvas.

Cooking helps preserve some foods, allowing us to reserve today's bounty for the scarcity of tomorrow. Cooking also makes some foods safer to eat. Cooking intensifies the nutritive value of some foods while making other nutrients more easily absorbed.

Yet cooking also can destroy the nutritional value of certain foods. Certain types of cooking also can make healthy food harmful.

The Philosophy of the Cooking Cardiologist

Julia Child created a guiltless kitchen. She showed us that even most expert chef can have a recipe flop and how to combine the science of experimentation with the creativity of artistry. A chef is a scientist, seeking to best blend the nutrition that supports and sustains life. A chef also is an artist painting a canvas of flavors to produce a recipe. Food is art; it is the expression of self.

As the Cooking Cardiologist, I believe that was the message that Julia Child conveyed. Of course, like all chefs, she believed that if something was "bad" for you, then "don't eat as much." However, restraint is not easy. My philosophy is simple, "If you know how to cook right, then you will know how to eat right."

Cool Cooking

As a general rule, high temperature cooking destroys the nutritional value of food. It also can cause certain foods to become harmful, generating potentially damaging compounds that promote inflammation, cancer, and cardiovascular disease.[134, 135]

Numerous studies have associated grilled and fried meats with an elevated risk of cancer, including breast, prostate, and colon.[136,137,138] The studies emphasize that cancer risks may not be associated with meat specifically, but rather with well-done, overdone, deep fried meats and the blackening or charring associated with high temperature or direct flame cooking.

Anything cooked with lots of water will maintain a relatively low heat. As the water reaches the 212 degree boiling point, it will steam, taking the heat with it. Steaming, stewing, poaching, and soup-making are great ways to cook any number of foods, often enhancing their nutritional value. Remember though, as foods dehydrate as they cook, temperatures will rise. Take care to avoid high heat.

Temperatures below 325 degrees are still considered low heat cooking. Above 325 degrees, the challenge posed by heat often depends on the food itself.

Antioxidants, Plant Sterols and Cooking Methods

- Baked, microwaved, simmered or raw, wild blueberries deliver the same antioxidant capacity.[139]
- Similar results were found for carrots and red cabbage as well as celery, beets, and garlic.[140,141,142]
- Cooking actually increases the antioxidant content of tomatoes.[143]
- Cooking green beans, other than boiling, will increase the antioxidant level. With boiling, the antioxidants are left behind in the water.[144]
- Spices can preserve the antioxidant levels of other cooked foods Turmeric has been shown to preserve antioxidant levels of cooking vegetables.[145]
- Plant sterols maintain stability when heated. Cooking broad beans, celery, cabbage, carrots, cauliflower, onion, and peppers increases the levels of plant sterols that can be used to block the absorption of cholesterol.[146]

When Good Fats Go Bad

Cooking in oil poses health challenges. Oils have a smoke point, a temperature that causes the chemical composition to breakdown rapidly and delivers unpleasant flavors. Different oils will start to smoke and burn at different temperatures. Unrefined corn and soy oils have a smoke point of 320 degrees. Extra virgin olive oil has a smoke point of 325 degrees, making it good for salads or light saute. Refined oils can handle a higher heat (See Figure 8.1).

Overheated oils contribute to the development of compounds known as free radicals, one or more atoms with at least one unpaired electron that make it unstable and highly reactive. Free radicals can damage cells and can accelerate the progression of cancer, cardiovascular disease, and other diseases. This is true not only for the unhealthy saturated and trans fats, but also the healthy monounsaturated and polyunsaturated fats. Free radicals are probably more dangerous than trans fats. And as the food approaches the smoke point, oils already may be starting to break down.

But oils, heated for extended periods of times at temperatures below their smoke point, also degrade, just more slowly.

One study found that reused cooking oil negatively affects the arteries' ability to open four hours after a meal, while the same meal cooked in fresh oil did not.[150] Rather than detecting a significant difference between the fresh fat and lowfat meals, the meal made in reused oils had an adverse impact on the arteries. Researchers continue to explore the potential impact of how degraded oil hinders the body's natural ability to regulate inflammation and harm arterial health.

Tips from the Cooking Cardiologist: Wok On!

Once a trendy shower or wedding gift, the wok seems to have since fallen out of favor. But stir frying in a wok remains an excellent technique for cooking greens and other vegetables with some meats, fish, or shellfish.

Stir frying occurs in a flash and requires high heat and a good quality wok pan. Because it is fast cooking, have everything ready, garlic chopped, fresh ginger grated, vegetables ready to go, and thinly sliced meat, chicken, or shellfish. Follows are steps for wok cooking:

1. Place the wok on high heat, and when it is hot, add no more than 2 tablespoons of oil with a high smoke point, such as teaseed oil. Do not use olive oil since its smoke point is too low. After a few moments, test the oil with a small amount of the aromatics (herbs or spices with a distinct aroma). If the wok sizzles, the oil is ready.

2. Then, add the aromatics, such as ginger or garlic. In less than a minute, they will begin to release their flavor and aroma, and you can begin to add the vegetables and meat in the order of their cooking times; those taking the longest are added first.

3. Stir, lift, and toss the ingredients until they are evenly cooked without scorching. Ingredients may be removed once they are cooked and can be returned to the wok after the rest of the recipe has absorbed a portion or all of the liquid.

4. Add the liquid ingredients and seasoning. For thinly sliced or shredded dishes, turn down the heat for a few minutes while the flavors combine, adjust the seasoning, and serve.

5. For dishes with tougher or larger ingredients, place a lid over the wok and adjust the temperature to maintain a simmer so that the food steams until it has absorbed a portion or all of the liquid. Then return any ingredients that were removed, adjust the seasoning, stir quickly, and serve.

Oil Type	Smoke Point	MUFA (g)	PUFA (g)	Omega-3 ALA	SatFat (g)	TranFat (g)	Plant Sterols (mg)	Description and Usage
Canola Refined	425° F	8.9	4.0	1.3	1.0	0.0	92.0	Neutral flavor, good for baking
Flax Seed Oil	225° F	2.7	9.0	7.0	1.3	0.0	0.0	Generally used as a supplement, not for cooking
Grape Seed Oil	420° F	2.2	9.5	0.0	1.3	0.0	24.0	Light, neutral flavor, sauteing
Olive Oil (Extra Virgin)	325° F	10.0	1.4	0.1	2.0	0.0	30.0	Nuanced flavors depending on source & quality; Ideal for salads, pestos, light sauteing
Olive Oil Pure	400° F	10.0	1.4	0.1	2.0	0.0	30.0	Mild & tolerant to low to medium heats
Rice Bran Oil	490° F	5.4	4.8	0.2	2.7	0.0	162.0	One of two great high temperature oils, neutral flavor, good source of plant sterols
Teaseed Oil	485° F	7.0	3.0	0.1	3.0	0.0	14.0	One of two great high temperature oils, neutral flavor

Figure 8.1 Using the Right Oils for the Right Recipes

Tips from the Cooking Cardiologist -- Induction Cooking

An induction cooker uses an induction coil to heat a ferromagnetic pan from an oscillating electromagnetic field. At least that is the scientific explanation. To put it more simply, it is cooking with magnetic waves. There's no flame; only the pan heats up. Compared to a conventional electric burner, induction cooking is faster and more efficient.

Gas is approximately 40 percent efficient, a conventional electric stove top is about 55 percent while induction cooking is 90 percent efficient. The temperature control is precise and the pan's temperature is constantly monitored by the unit, making it impossible to overheat oil.

Portable units that plug into any outlet are now being made and full cooktops can be installed permanently. Induction cookers also produces magnetic waves. They should not be used by those with an implantable electronic pacemaker/defibrillator.

Induction cooking requires a ferromagnetic pan. Testing the pan is relatively easy: if a magnet sticks to it, it is induction compatible.

When Good Carbs Go Bad

If you like your bread well-toasted, consider an alternative. When carbohydrates are heated to high temperatures and browned, as with baking, frying, or toasting, compounds known as acrylamides can form. Industrially, acrylamides are used in wastewater treatment, papermaking, ore processing, dyes, and the manufacture of permanent press fabrics.

In foods, acrylamides have been most widely associated with elevated cancer risks. These compounds also have been linked with the inflammation that can contribute to the development of arterial plaque.[147]

Acrylamides are not found in boiled, steamed, or uncooked foods. With other cooking methods, acrylamides have been shown to be lower in home cooked foods than in processed foods. ⌧

Combine Your Cooking Techniques

You need not completely abandon the great tastes imparted by sautéing, barbequing, grilling, and broiling. You just need to use them carefully and not throughout the entire process. This is a technique known as combination cooking.

Start by marinating meats beforehand and blending spices into your recipes to reduce the level of inflammatory compounds created during cooking.

Allow lower temperature cooking methods – lower temperature oven roasting, stewing, steaming and poaching to do most of the cooking. You might start with a hotter flame to sear and impart a delicious flavor, and finish with lower temperatures. Alternatively, these lower temperature cooking methods can be utilized upfront, finishing with the hotter flame or higher heat.

When cooking on the barbeque, complete most of the cooking at a lower temperature on top of the stove, in the oven, or, if on the grill, to the side of the direct flames. Finish over the coals.

You can also utilize a wooden plank available in many kitchen supply store to impart a smoky flavor. Soaked in water for an hour, the plank will not burn when placed on the hot grill and will keep the food from direct exposure to high heat and flames. The smoky flavor from the hot coals will still develop. When using the plank, use a dry spice rub rather than highly sweetened sauces. The evaporating water from the plank will prevent the rub from burning while helping the spice flavors penetrate. Spice blends also help control the inflammatory impact of cooked meats. The soapstone discussed on page 190 in Chapter Nine can be used as an alternative to the plank.

Combination cooking also can work to preserve the more healthful qualities of unsaturated fats while allowing reduction in the amount of calorie dense oils. For example, try cooking vegetables using a "water sauté," which is much more flavorful than steaming.

Sauté onions or garlic in a small amount of oil. This refines their more pungent qualities. At the same time, add some of your favorite spices. A quick sauté will add zest to the spice and allow the flavors to blend. Watch the pan carefully. Do not let the oil smoke. Keep it on a low to medium temperature. Then add a bit of balsamic vinegar, Marsala wine or vermouth, or tomato or fruit juice. Add the vegetables quickly. Toss in the pan and cover. Let the flavored moisture cook the vegetables through.

Here is another trick. When the vegetables are done, remove them from the pan. You can now reduce the liquid, creating a flavorful, nutrient rich sauce – many of the vegetables' nutrients leach into the water during the cooking process and too often are thrown away. Basically reducing a liquid means evaporating a portion of it. This is done by simmering or boiling the liquid so that the water evaporates and concentrates. It's not an exact science, so if a recipe says "reduce by half," simmer or boil it until there is about half as much liquid as there was in the beginning. Combine different spices, vegetables, and liquids to bring great taste and balance to a meal.

Chapter 9
FROM TEXT TO TABLE

Food is never just food. It's also a way of getting at something else; who we are, who we have been and who we want to be.

Molly Wizenberg, 2009

Perhaps this last chapter should be labeled as the first. It has the recipes that you have been waiting to read. Maybe you skipped the science that lead us to healthy eating foundation of the other chapters. Regardless, these recipes will excite your healthy culinary journey. We will explore some of the culinary elements and recipes of the Mediterranean region. Starting in Spain, we will journey to France and then to Greece, Lebanon, and end in North Africa with Moroccan cuisine. Our goal is make these traditional foods heart healthier and easier to prepare.

This chapter ends with a few additional recipes and cooking techniques that support delicious heart healthy eating.

The recipes offer only a few of the available options. They can serve as a starting point, providing instruction as to how you can use mostly healthy ingredients to make healthier recipes. You then can match these recipes to make even healthier meals, enjoying the artistry and experimentation of creating dishes that fit your tastes and lifestyle. And while countless recipes and cookbooks are available, you might start with your current stockpile of recipes and consider doing a simple makeover, using the information found in this book. Simple changes, big results.

"Flexible" Recipes for Better Health

Many of the following recipes are flexible, selected to adapt to meet your taste preferences and personal philosophies. They are designed to help identify the dishes that can be used along your journey to heart healthier eating.

We look to dishes that you can evolve. It can be very difficult to move from being a "red meat and fried potato" or "macaroni and cheese" eater to someone who relishes "steamed greens and brown rice." A beefy chili topped with cheese and sour cream can become a bean and vegetable chili served with only a sprinkle of cheese, chopped green onion, and tomato. The cooking techniques are similar, the seasonings and taste can be maintained. The important difference: the heart healthy profile has improved.

Next, become comfortable making heart healthy flexible recipes. Make sure the basic ingredients found in your heart healthy recipes are always in your pantry. Put these recipes into your cooking rotation. Rather than being used once in a while, they should become a part of your weekly – if not daily -- eating patterns.

Another challenge may be that all types of eaters come together to enjoy a meal. The diverse eating philosophies within the family can make cooking a meal at home more difficult. Children often drive what we put on the kitchen table.

They are impressionable and the first line of fire for advertising gimmicks like a quick pizza delivery, takeout tonight, and burgers from the arches. Be careful of their demands. You need to guide the family in the proper direction. Lack of time, preparation, costs, convenience, and the multitude of food preferences may tempt you to buy food on the run, piecemeal the dinner, and supersize the amounts. But the fast food industry isn't entirely to blame. We are still the consumers.

Make Balanced, Satisfying Meals

Our recipes are only a starting point for your heart healthy cooking. Typically, one dish does not make a satisfying meal. At home, a satisfying meal, even one with a single course, will include two or three dishes --meat, potatoes, and the salad; the protein, the starch, and the vegetable. A multicourse meal, like many enjoy in a restaurant or during a household celebration, may offer four or five different dishes, plus bread.

So often, the efforts to move to healthier eating are undone by the failure to recognize that the meal requires multiple dishes. The meat dish, for instance, may be dropped, leaving only the starch and the vegetable. In smart and delicious eating, start by maintaining the same number of dishes that you would typically enjoy. Find the combination of foods that will satisfy your senses and satisfy your hunger. Remember, though, that we no longer look to the protein, starch, vegetable balance. You are looking to achieve a new balance on the plate --- a balance that increases the levels of foods that help and minimize foods that harm. Use what you have learned throughout this book to help guide you on this journey.

Meals with the Cooking Cardiologist

By combining dishes, you can bring a heart healthy balance to every meal. Make sure to eat foods mostly from the plant kingdom and some from the sea to insure that you are enjoying adequate levels of helpful nutrients. Remember to build towards the basic rules of heart healthy eating:

- Fruit with every meal
- Greens with lunch and dinner
- Use whole grains and beans to satisfy and add fiber
- Include brightly colored vegetables to add beauty, antioxidants, and flavor

Build your meals around these rules and you will stay in balance. Everything else falls to the simple love of delicious foods.

Salt: A Grain of Advice

However much salt you put into a recipe, the salt shaker still sits on the table. Family members and friends choose how much sodium they consume with the meal. As you move toward heart healthier eating, your tastes can change. You may find that you need lower levels of salt for taste satisfaction. In this light, our recipes generally do not define the amount of salt to use. We simply reference "salt to taste."

For some, the recipes are delicious without any added salt. Others will reach for the salt shaker.

As part of your cooking experiments, define the amount you require and work down from there. Also recall that the sodium in salt affects people differently. Salt sensitive people will see a sharper rise in blood pressure from sodium than those who are not salt sensitive. Your focus on salt reduction in relationship to other foods that might cause harm, like calorie-rich, cholesterol-increasing oils or blood-sugar-spiking carbohydrates, can vary with your risk factors, but remember optimizing heart health still looks to shifting your eating balance from all foods that harm to the foods that help. For most, elevated salt levels fall into the category of foods that harm.

Enjoy Healthy Cooking!

Cooking should be an opportunity to create something unique and delicious and to relax. Certainly this will not be the case for every meal. While sometimes it's just a matter of getting food on the table, look for a way to make each meal just a bit special or different. Try a touch of a new spice or something seasonal – a fruit or vegetable not normally eaten that might be particularly delicious this time of year. Combining vegetables, spices, and sometimes fruits that can be varied from season to season provide nutrient-rich, low-calorie foods that add flavor and enjoyment.

Of course, not every dish will be a masterpiece. In fact, some may be downright unsatisfying. But each time you prepare a meal, look for something exceptional that will add to the fun and the challenge – whether in the ingredients, the preparation, or the manner in which it is enjoyed and shared.

For the Heart of Spain

For many Americans, two dishes define Spanish cuisine: Gazpacho -- cold, fresh, and raw vegetable soup -- and paella, a full-flavored rice dish combining vegetables, seafood, and meats.

From one region in Spain to another, these dishes take on their own unique qualities. Using a general recipe, their specific ingredients can be varied based on the seasonal availability.

Overall, gazpacho and paella have a useful place in heart healthy eating. Admittedly, we take some creative license with both. We adapted traditional gazpacho recipes to make them easier to prepare. We altered the paella recipes to utilize a more nutritious grain as opposed to the traditional white rice. The paella has an option of a vegan, shellfish, and shellfish and meat version.

Together, these two dishes make for a well-matched, healthy meal, delivering substantial levels of antioxidants, fibers, and complex carbohydrates, lots of vegetables, and a healthier grain. You will also get some Omega-3s if you add the shellfish to the paella. Additionally, the tomato-based gazpacho has a high level of potassium.

To complete the meal, serve the paella with a steamed or lightly sautéed green vegetable.

Gazpachos

Originating from the Andalusia region of Spain, this chilled soup is a summertime favorite. Traditional gazpacho is made from tomatoes and fresh garden vegetables such as peppers, onions, cucumbers, garlic, and vinegar. A version from the American Southwest adds cilantro.

A nutrient-rich, satisfying salad-in-a-glass, cool and complex gazpachos blend the taste of vegetables, spices, and herbs. The preparation of traditional gazpachos can be time-consuming. With a blender or food processor, the Kardea recipes only take about 10-20 minutes. All can be prepared quickly with minimal mess, making a perfect weekend lunch, first course, or part of a lighter summer meal. Make extra gazpacho for a great mid-afternoon snack!

Note for all gazpacho recipes: A food processor makes preparation very simple and gives you somewhat better control over consistency (a blender also works, but it may take a few batches). Chop vegetables (and fruits) into large chunks; the key is to avoid pureeing the mixture. Use the "pulse" button to coarsely chop the melon and vegetables. Gazpacho is best prepared fresh but earlier in the day to allow flavors to develop. Chill well, serve as a drink or as a soup with garnishes -- chopped, fresh green or red peppers, tomatoes, cucumbers, avocados, or scallions -- in cold margarita or martini glasses.

Tomato Gazpacho *(Serves 4)*

16   ounces tomato juice - low sodium
2   medium cucumbers, peeled, coarsely chopped
12   ounce jar of roasted red peppers with liquid
1   medium onion
2-3   cloves garlic
2   tbsp virgin olive oil
1/2   cup fresh cilantro
1/4   cup fresh parsley
2   tbsp vinegar (white, rice, or balsamic)
Hot sauce to taste

Additional spice options:
1/2   tsp cumin
1/2   tsp smoked paprika
2   Tbsp green olives
1   Tbsp capers

Nutrition Facts

Calories (kcal) 90, Protein (g) 2, Carbohydrates (g) 10, Dietary Fiber (g) 3, Soluble Fiber (g) 0, Total Sugars (g) 6, Fat (g) 5, Saturated Fat (g) 1, Mono Fat (g) 3, Poly Fat (g) 1, Trans Fatty Acid (g) 0, Cholesterol (mg) 0, Calcium (mg) 35, Magnesium (mg) 13, Potassium (mg) 535, Sodium (mg) 55, Omega 3 Fatty Acid (mg) 0

Watermelon Gazpacho *(Serves 4)*

6   cups cubed watermelon, seeds removed
1   cup coarsely chopped peeled English cucumber
1/2   cup coarsely chopped yellow bell pepper
1/3   cup chopped green onions
3   Tbsp chopped fresh mint
3   Tbsp fresh lime juice
1/2   tsp hot sauce
1   garlic clove, minced
1   cup tart berry or pomegranate juice
Salt to taste

Additional Instructions:

Combine one-half of watermelon and entire cucumber, bell pepper, onions, mint, lime juice, hot sauce, and garlic in a food processor. Pulse to coarsely chop, usually two or three brief pulses. Place in a large bowl. Add the juice. Chop the remaining watermelon and add to the mixture. Chill thoroughly.

Nutrition Facts

Calories (kcal) 130, Protein (g) 3, Carbohydrates (g) 32, Dietary Fiber (g) 3, Soluble Fiber (g) 0, Total Sugars (g) 25, Fat (g) 1, Saturated Fat (g) 0 Mono Fat (g) 0, Poly Fat (g) 0, Trans Fatty Acid (g) 0, Cholesterol (mg) 0, Calcium (mg) 60, Magnesium (mg) 45, Potassium (mg) 650 Sodium (mg) 15, Omega 3 Fatty Acid (mg) 0

Mango Gazpacho *(Serves 4)*

This recipe is a twist on the original using fresh mangos and a prepared mango puree found in the juice section of most groceries or natural food stores. This chilled soup is loaded with Vitamin C and colorful antioxidants. Serve chilled with garnishes, in hollowed out green peppers or chilled martini glasses.

1	mango, chopped
16	ounces mango puree juice
1	bunch of green onions, chopped
1	red bell pepper chopped
1	yellow bell pepper, chopped
2	Tbsp chopped cilantro
1/4	cup rice vinegar
8	green peppers, chilled, tops removed and seeds removed, using these as "bowls"
1	jalapeño chopped
1	seedless cucumber, sliced in strips and lightly drizzled with rice vinegar for garnish

Juice of one lime

Cilantro leaves for garnish
Salt and pepper to taste
Combine all ingredients into a large bowl. Mix well.

Nutrition Facts

Calories (kcal) 210, Protein (g) 5, Carbohydrates (g) 51, Dietary Fiber (g) 9, Soluble Fiber (g) 1, Total Sugars (g) 38, Fat (g) 1, Saturated Fat (g) 0, Mono Fat (g) 0, Poly Fat (g) 0, Trans Fatty Acid (g) 0, Cholesterol (mg) 0, Calcium (mg) 75, Magnesium (mg) 45, Potassium (mg) 940, Sodium (mg) 16, Omega 3 Fatty Acid (mg) 10

Barley Pilaf/Barley Paella

While the Spanish have used white rice as the basis of paella for over 500 years, the Kardea barley pilaf recipe builds an even healthier version of this great dish.

Everyday Barley Pilaf *(Serves 4)*

1   cup well rinsed pearled barley
2   cups water
1   small onion, chopped small
2   Tbsp pure olive oil
1/2 tsp turmeric
Salt and pepper to taste

Additional spice options:

If serving the pilaf with lean meats or roasted root vegetables, try adding spices such as curry or cumin. For serving with fish, add 2 teaspoons of fresh grated ginger and 1/2 cup of currants.

Rinse barley until water is no longer cloudy and runs clear. Set aside to drain.

Heat a saucepan over medium heat. Add olive oil and chopped onion. Sauté for a few minutes.

Add rinsed barley to the pan and sauté for five minutes, stirring regularly and making sure that barley does not burn or stick to bottom of pan. Add turmeric and then water to the hot barley and stir. Cover, lower heat, and cook until tender but still a bit chewy (about 30 minutes).

Remove cover and on very low heat, let steam escape. Periodically fluff to prevent sticking to bottom of pan. Serve when barley appears about the consistency of steamed rice. The turmeric also gives the barley a beautiful yellow color, accenting the visual appeal of the entire meal.

Nutrition Facts

Calories (kcal) 215, Protein (g) 5, Carbohydrates (g) 41, Dietary Fiber (g) 8, Soluble Fiber (g) 2, Total Sugars (g) 1, Fat (g) 4, Saturated Fat (g) 1 Mono Fat (g) 3, Poly Fat (g) 1, Trans Fatty Acid (g) 0, Cholesterol (mg) 0, Calcium (mg) 20, Magnesium (mg) 40, Potassium (mg) 280, Sodium (mg) 5, Omega 3 Fatty Acid (mg) 0

Barley Paella: The Vegan Version *(Serves 4)*

1	cup well rinsed pearled barley
2	cups water
1	small onion-chopped small
2	tbsp extra virgin olive oil
1	cup peas, fresh or frozen
1/2	fresh red pepper, thinly sliced into rings*
1/2	cup roasted pepper, cut into wide strips (fresh roasted or jarred)
1	cup artichoke hearts, quartered
1	tbsp capers
1/2	cup white wine
1/4	cup chopped green olives
1	tsp smoked paprika
1/2	tsp turmeric
1/2	tsp saffron
1/2	cup fresh chopped parsley
Salt to taste	

Optional Ingredient
1 cup cooked chick peas

Rinse barley until water is no longer cloudy and runs clear. Set aside to drain.

Heat an ovenproof pan over medium heat. Add olive oil, chopped onion, and red pepper rings. Sauté for a few minutes. Remove pepper rings.

Add rinsed barley to the pan and sauté for five minutes, stirring regularly and making sure that barley does not burn or stick to bottom of pan. Add turmeric and saffron, and then water to the hot barley. Stir until the yellow color of the spice is dispersed through the pan. Cover, lower heat, and cook for 25 minutes. While the barley is cooking on the stove top, pre-heat oven to 350 degrees.

Blend smoked paprika with chopped roasted peppers and chickpeas (if desired), add white wine and then gently blend into the barley. Layer red pepper rings, artichoke quarters, capers and chopped olives on top of barley. Cover and bake in oven for 20-30 minutes.

Nutrition Facts

Calories (kcal) 230, Protein (g) 6, Carbohydrates (g) 37, Dietary Fiber (g) 10, Soluble Fiber (g) 2, Total Sugars (g) 3, Fat (g) 6, Saturated Fat (g) 1, Mono Fat (g) 4 Poly Fat (g) 1, Trans Fatty Acid (g) 0, Cholesterol (mg) 0, Calcium (mg) 40, Magnesium (mg) 45, Potassium (mg) 285, Sodium (mg) 170, Omega 3 Fatty Acid (mg) 0

Barley Paella with Shellfish (Serves 6)

8	shrimp, deveined, tails on
8	mussels
8	claims
2	cloves garlic
1	bay leaf
1/2	tbsp olive oil
1/2	cup white wine
1/2	cup water

In a separate pan, heat oil and then add garlic. Cook for only about a minute or two, making sure that the garlic does not brown.

Add wine, water, and bay leaf. Bring to a boil. Add shrimp, mussels, and clams. Cook for 2 - 3 minutes.

Add the shellfish in the same way as vegetables in the vegan version. Pour cooking liquid from the shellfish over the barley to add flavor and nutrients. Finish by layering in red pepper rings, capers, artichoke quarters, and chopped olives.

Nutrition Facts

Calories (kcal) 270, Protein (g) 13, Carbohydrates (g) 39, Dietary Fiber (g) 10, Soluble Fiber (g) 2, Total Sugars (g) 3, Fat (g) 6, Saturated Fat (g) 1, Mono Fat (g) 4,Poly Fat (g) 1, Trans Fatty Acid (g) 0, Cholesterol (mg) 25, Calcium (mg) 60, Magnesium (mg) 60, Potassium (mg) 435 Sodium (mg) 250, Omega 3 Fatty Acid (mg) 300

Barley Paella with Shellfish & Meat (Serves 6)

Some paellas add chicken and chorizo, a Spanish sausage. Cut 8 ounces of skinless chicken breast in 2 inch pieces and one chorizo into ½ inch wide slices. Lightly brown in pan while heating the oil and before adding the garlic. Then follow the fish preparation above.

Nutrition Facts

Calories (kcal) 360, Protein (g) 23, Carbohydrates (g) 39, Dietary Fiber (g) 10 Soluble Fiber (g) 2, Total Sugars (g) 3, Fat (g) 11, Saturated Fat (g) 3, Mono Fat (g) 6, Poly Fat (g) 1, Trans Fatty Acid (g) 0, Cholesterol (mg) 55, Calcium (mg) 65, Magnesium (mg) 65, Potassium (mg) 540, Sodium (mg) 400, Omega 3 Fatty Acid (mg) 300

For the Heart of France

Julia Child's beef bourguignon is a rich stew that delights the senses and warms the soul. And as a stew, it incorporates lower-temperature, liquid-based cooking with the antioxidants of red wine, and selected herbs and vegetables. A traditional beef bourguignon also delivers a considerable amount of red meat, butter, and bacon.

The culinary spirit of this dish is crafted into the Kardea vegan mushroom bourguignon. Meat lovers can enjoy Kardea vegetable bourguignon with beef. This version builds on the concept that red meat should not play a center role in the recipe but rather as an ingredient that brings flavor, aroma, and texture to a meal.

Serve with the Kardea chickpea crepe recipe -- a gluten-free source of fiber and protein -- and a green salad with a herb-enriched vinaigrette.

Mushroom Bourguignon (Vegan) (Serves 4)

2	tbsp olive oil
1	large carrot chopped
1	large onion chopped
4	cloves garlic, diced
1/2	tsp dried thyme
1	bay leaf
1 1/2	cups red wine
2	pounds Portobello mushrooms, cut in 1/2 inch thick slices and then halved.
2	tbsp dried porcini mushrooms

8-10 small whole onions
2   cups butternut squash, 1-2 inch cubes
1   cup parsnips, halved and sliced
Salt to taste

Bring a large pan to a medium heat, add oil, coating the entire base. Add the carrots and onion to the pan; sauté for 3-4 minutes. Add garlic, thyme, bay leaf, and wine. Cover and simmer on low heat for 20 minutes. Next add small onions, butternut squash, and parsnips. Cover again and raise temperature to a medium heat and cook for about 10 minutes. Add mushrooms and cook with cover off for another 10 minutes.

Nutritional Facts

Calories 219, Protein (g) 7, Carbohydrates (g) 30, Dietary Fiber (g) 6, Soluble Fiber (g) 0, Total Sugars (g) 10, Fat (g) 5, Saturated Fat (g) 1, Mono Fat (g) 3, Poly Fat (g) 1, Trans Fatty Acid (g) 0, Cholesterol (mg) 0, Calcium (mg) 80, Iron (mg) 3, Magnesium (mg) 55, Potassium (mg) 1210, Sodium (mg) 30, Omega 3 Fatty Acid (g) 0

Vegetable Bourguignon with Beef (Serves 6)

1 1/2 lb lean stewing beef cut in 2 inch cubes
2   tbsp teaseed, canola or olive oil
1   large carrot chopped
1   large onion chopped
2   cloves garlic, diced
1/2 tsp dried thyme
1   bay leaf
1 1/2 cups red wine
1   cup low sodium tomato juice
8-10 small white onions
2   cups butternut squash, 1-2 inch cubes
1   cup parsnips, halved and sliced
1   pound fresh mushrooms
Salt and pepper to taste

Bring a large pan to a medium heat, add oil, coating the entire base. Add meat, making sure that the pan is not too crowded. Brown on all sides and remove meat from pan with a slotted spoon. In same hot pan, add the carrots and onion to the pan; cook off excess moisture and sauté for 3-4 minutes. Return beef to the pan and add wine, thyme and bay leaf. Cover and simmer on low heat for 1 ½ hours. Make sure the meat stays substantially covered with liquid.

Add small onions, butternut squash, and parsnips. Raise temperature to a medium heat and cook for about 5 minutes. Add mushrooms and optional beans and cook with cover off for another 15-20 minutes.

Nutrition Facts

Calories (kcal) 380, Protein (g) 29, Carbohydrates (g) 33, Dietary Fiber (g) 8, Soluble Fiber (g) 0, Total Sugars (g) 8, Fat (g) 10, Saturated Fat (g) 2, Mono Fat (g) 5, Poly Fat (g) 2, Trans Fatty Acid (g) 0, Cholesterol (mg) 48, Calcium (mg) 95, Iron (mg) 4, Magnesium (mg) 50, Potassium (mg) 800, Sodium (mg) 370, Omega 3 Fatty Acid (g) 0

Chickpea (Garbanzo Bean) Crepes (Serves 4)

1 1/2 cups cold water
3   tbsp teaseed or rice bran oil
2   cups chickpea flour
1/2   tsp salt
Freshly ground black pepper

Spice options (add one or more of the following):
1 tsp cumin
1 tsp rosemary
1 tsp freshly ground fennel seed
1 tsp freshly ground caraway seed

Preheat the oven to 450 degrees. Sift the chickpea flour into a bowl. In a separate large bowl, whisk together water, olive oil, and salt. Add chickpea flour, a little at a time, whisking in completely to make a batter. Set batter aside.

Place a large, oven-safe skillet in the hot oven for 4-5 minutes. Remove pan carefully – it will be very hot. Quickly add enough of a higher temperature oil (such as teaseed or rice bran) so it covers the bottom of the pan. Working quickly, add a ½ cup of the batter to the pan, swirling it around to fill the pan in an even thin layer. Put in oven and cook 5-7 minutes till browned a bit around the edges. Remove from oven. Flip. It should be golden brown on the bottom.

Cut the heated crepe into wedges and serve with the bourguignon.

Nutrition Facts

Calories (kcal) 270, Protein (g) 10, Carbohydrates (g) 27, Dietary Fiber (g) 5, Soluble Fiber (g) 0, Total Sugars (g) 5, Fat (g) 13, Saturated Fat (g) 2, Mono Fat (g) 6, Poly Fat (g) 4, Trans Fatty Acid (g) 0, Cholesterol (mg) 0, Calcium (mg) 20, Iron (mg) 2, Magnesium (mg) 85, Potassium (mg) 480, Sodium (mg) 165, Omega 3 Fatty Acid (g) 0

Ratatouille (Serves 4)

Ratatouille, a traditional recipe from the south of France, recently has reemerged due in part to the 2007 film *Ratatouille*.

A medley of tossed vegetables, typically zucchini, eggplant, tomatoes, peppers, onions, garlic and herbs, ratatouille-like dishes can be found in other parts of the Mediterranean: in a Maltese version called kapunata, an Italian version known as caponata, and the Spanish dish pisto. Indian cooking also has brindil bhaji, its own version of ratatouille.

For the film, Chef Thomas Keller was given a task of transforming this French countryside dish into a creation that would please even the most difficult food critic. Instead of sautéing the vegetables on the stovetop, they were thinly sliced and arranged, overlapping in a skillet beneath a roasted pepper-based sauce.

We have taken a few liberties to make home cooking easier. In the movie, each vegetable is carefully cut into thin, uniform rounds and then carefully layered in the pan. This makes for a beautiful presentation, but is time-consuming in real life. Instead, we slice the zucchini, squash, and eggplant lengthwise. A mandolin (see below) can be used for slicing both ways. The sauces have also been adapted to use standard items such as a jar of roasted red peppers and a can of salt-free tomatoes, reducing sauce preparation time.

The Kardea version starts as a vegan recipe. Another twist involves a few ounces of gruyere cheese.

The Cooking Cardiologist: Making Ratatouille "Sing"

Along with other dishes, preparation of ratatouille can be made faster, easier, and elegant with a mandolin. We're not talking about the musical instrument, but rather a cooking utensil used for slicing and cutting food. The mandolin consists of two parallel working surfaces, one of which can be adjusted in height.

The mandolin can quickly slice or julienne food in several uniform widths and thicknesses. It also slices and makes waffle and crinkle cuts with firmer vegetables and fruits. Along with a food processor, the mandolin is a terrific time saving tool for the plant-based chef. But take care to use the safety features; your fingers should not be part of any recipe!

1 medium zucchini sliced lengthwise, 1/8 inch thick
1 medium eggplant sliced lengthwise, 1/8 inch thick
1 yellow squash sliced lengthwise, 1/8 inch thick
1 medium onion, sliced into 1/8 inch rings,
1 small onion, quartered
1 - 12 oz jar roasted red peppers
1 - 8 oz can salt-free tomatoes
1 clove garlic
1 tsp. dried thyme
2 tbsp olive oil
Salt to taste

Optional Ingredients
4 ounces gruyere, sliced thin
1/4 cup kalamata olives, pitted

On a baking sheet, place onions slices into in a 350 degree oven for 10 minutes. Turn and let cook for an additional 5 minutes. No oil is necessary.

While the sliced onions are cooking, combine in a food processor or blender the roasted pepper with it liquid, the tomatoes, the quartered onion, olive oil, garlic, and thyme. Pulse until pureed.

Cover the bottom of an ovenproof pan with the vegetable puree. Layer in the eggplant. Cover with more of the puree. Add a layer of squash and cooked onion rings and cover with more puree and optional kalamata olives. Add another layer of eggplant and cover again. Cover and place in the 350 degree oven for about 1 ¼ hours. Remove lid and continue to cook for another 20 minutes. Remove from oven and let cool for at least 15 minutes before serving.

If you add the gruyere and olives, use about ¼ to $^1/_3$ of each to each layer. Both the gruyere and the kalamata olives deliver saltiness.

Nutrition Facts without Cheese
Calories (kcal) 110, Protein (g) 3, Carbohydrates (g) 16, Dietary Fiber (g) 6, Soluble Fiber (g) 0, Total Sugars (g) 8, Fat (g) 5, Saturated Fat (g) 1, Mono Fat (g) 3, Poly Fat (g) 1, Trans Fatty Acid (g) 0, Cholesterol (mg) 0, Calcium (mg) 35, Iron (mg) 2, Magnesium (mg) 40, Potassium (mg) 660, Sodium (mg) 30, Omega 3 Fatty Acid (g) 0

Nutrition Facts with Cheese
Calories (kcal) 210, Protein (g) 9, Carbohydrates (g) 16, Dietary Fiber (g) 6, Soluble Fiber (g) 0, Total Sugars (g) 8, Fat (g) 13, Saturated Fat (g) 5, Mono Fat (g) 7, Poly Fat (g) 1, Trans Fatty Acid (g) 0, Cholesterol (mg) 21, Calcium (mg) 230, Iron (mg) 2, Magnesium (mg) 45, Potassium (mg) 670, Sodium (mg) 90, Omega 3 Fatty Acid (g) 0

For the Heart of Italy

During the period when "lowfat" was the focal point of healthy eating, pasta had a central role in evening meal planning and offered a quick, easy, and comforting dinner solution for the would-be health conscious eater. We have since realized that a meal dominated by white flour pasta triggers spikes in blood sugar.

Today, whole grain, higher fiber, or high protein pastas are healthier. Yet a big plate of whole grain pasta ladened with oil still falls well short of a well-balanced, well-matched meal.

Rather than letting pasta dominate, allow it to represent no more than a third to a half of the serving; beans or vegetables should play the leading role. Seafood can also be added. Or you can include some red meat for texture and flavor.

Pasta Fagioli (Serves 4)

Any bean can be used for this dish. All beans are good sources of the soluble fiber that helps to reduce cholesterol levels. Red beans in particular contain high levels of antioxidants. If you start with canned beans, this dish can be prepared in a total of about 50 minutes with only about 25 minutes of actual prep/chef time. If you plan ahead, start with the dried beans. They tend to have better flavor and are lower in sodium. Again, the principal of using meat to add flavor is incorporated as an optional ingredient.

2 cups cooked (or rinsed and drained canned) red beans
3 tbsp extra virgin olive oil (2 tbsp if using panchetta
    or bacon)
1 medium onion, chopped
1 medium green pepper, chopped
2 medium carrots, chopped
1 celery stalk, chopped
4 cloves fresh garlic, chopped
2 cups chopped plum tomatoes, fresh or canned with juice
1/2 cup good quality red wine
1/8 tsp red pepper flakes
2 Tbsp dried porcini mushroom, coarsely chopped
1/2 bay leaf
1/4 cup minced flat leaf (Italian) parsley
2 cups cooked pasta
Salt to taste

Optional ingredients:
4 thin slices of pancetta or two strips of bacon

Place a large, heavy saucepan or casserole dish over medium heat. If using pancetta or bacon, add first. Cook on each side for 1-2 minutes. Add olive oil, onion, garlic, carrots, pepper, and celery. Cover and cook over medium-low heat for 10-15 minutes, opening occasionally to stir.

Add tomatoes, wine, and bay leaf. Cover and simmer for another 20 minutes. Add beans, red pepper flakes, and porcini mushrooms. Cook until mushrooms are soft.

Combine one cup of this sauce with one cup of your favorite whole-grain or higher fiber pasta. Toss in parsley when ready to serve.

This recipe also has variations. Add roasted pepper to create a fagioli cacciatore (hunter's bean stew). Or serve it as an appetizer with a drizzle of olive oil and whole grain bread.

Nutrition Facts

Calories (kcal) 410, Protein (g) 15, Carbohydrates (g) 59, Dietary Fiber (g) 11, Soluble Fiber (g) 3, Total Sugars (g) 4, Fat (g) 12, Saturated Fat (g) 2, Mono Fat (g) 8, Poly Fat (g) 2, Trans Fatty Acid (g) 0, Cholesterol (mg) 0, Vitamin D - IU (IU) 0, Calcium (mg) 115, Iron (mg) 5, Magnesium (mg) 90, Potassium (mg) 995, Sodium (mg) 193, Omega 3 Fatty Acid (mg) 0

Walnut Basil Pesto *(Serves 12)*

You know it's really summer when large, aromatic bunches of basil show up in the farmer's market. Consisting of finely chopped basil with garlic, olive oil, pine nuts, parmesan cheese, and perhaps some parsley, traditional pesto also is high in fat and calories. When coupled with lots of white pasta, it can trigger a more intense glycemic response. The anti-inflammatory benefits of the herbs are overwhelmed, and the postprandial impact of meal can be intense.

But you can still enjoy pesto and pasta as long as it's balanced with other foods. Comprising only 1/3 of the meal, it can be enjoyed with a fresh seasonal salad, very light on the dressing, and 3-4 ounces of a poached, grilled, or slow-roasted fish or chicken. A steamed or water sautéed green vegetable can add balancing nutrients.

Also think of how you might use the pesto differently. Toss into a combination of chick peas, neatly diced fresh red and yellow peppers, and halved cherry tomatoes. Use as the spread in a roasted eggplant sandwich.

The Kardea pesto also is lighter than more traditional pesto recipes. We have refined a standard pesto recipe to improve its heart healthy qualities. Sautéed walnuts replace the parmesan cheese, reducing both the sodium and saturated fat levels. Walnuts, in particular, have been associated with heart health and help maintain the great pesto consistency. The pesto also freezes well and can be enjoyed throughout the winter.

4 cups fresh basil leaves, loosely packed
1 cup fresh parsley, loosely packed
1 cup walnuts
2/3 cup extra virgin olive oil
4 large cloves garlic, chopped

Heat a pan over low heat. When heated, add 1/3 cup of olive oil, 3 cloves of chopped garlic and all the walnuts. Sauté 2-4 minutes or until garlic is soft but not browned. You are only sautéing to remove the bite of the garlic and add nuttiness to the walnuts. Set aside and let cool.

In a food processor, add the second 1/3 cup of olive oil, the basil, the parsley and 1 clove of the fresh, chopped garlic. Blend with the sautéed walnuts.

The pesto is now ready for multiple uses.   If you love the parmesan cheese, sprinkle on top of the dish, do not blend in. In this way, the flavor will not get buried. You will be able to identify the taste with far less cheese.   Keep the meal in balance

To freeze, place about a half cup (enough for about a pound of pasta) in a small container. Cover with a thin coat of olive oil and freeze.

Nutrition Facts

Calories (kcal) 180, Protein (g) 2, Carbohydrates (g) 2, Dietary Fiber (g) 1, Soluble Fiber (g) 0, Total Sugars (g) 0, Fat (g) 19, Saturated Fat (g) 2, Mono Fat (g) 10, Poly Fat (g) 6, Trans Fatty Acid (g) 0, Cholesterol (mg) 0, Vitamin D - IU (IU) 0, Calcium (mg) 45, Iron (mg) 1, Magnesium (mg) 30, Potassium (mg) 115, Sodium (mg) 4, Omega 3 Fatty Acid (mg) 1000

Shrimp with Walnut Pesto and Vegetables (Serves 4)

8 jumbo shrimp, deveined, tail on
2 cups cherry or grape tomatoes, halved
2 small zucchinis, diced into 1 inch cubes
1 tbsp teaseed oil or other higher temperature oil
1/2 cup white wine
3 cloves garlic, chopped
3 cups cooked pasta
6 tbsp walnut basil pesto (see recipe on page 182)
1/4 cup, fresh parsley or fresh basil, chopped
Salt to taste

Optional Ingredients
1 cup cooked white beans
1/2 teaspoon fennel seed

Heat a pan to a medium heat, add olive oil and garlic and sauté for 2 minutes. Before the garlic browns, add zucchini, shrimp, optional ingredients (white beans and fennel seed), and the white wine. Cover tightly and cook for about 5 minutes. Add halved tomatoes and cook uncovered for another 5 minutes. Toss once or twice to insure that all ingredients are cooking evenly.

Toss the walnut basil pesto into the cooked pasta and then add the shrimp and vegetables.

Nutrition Facts

Calories (kcal) 735, Protein (g) 17, Carbohydrates (g) 46, Dietary Fiber (g) 7, Soluble Fiber (g) 1, Total Sugars (g) 5, Fat (g) 58, Saturated Fat (g) 7, Mono Fat (g) 29, Poly Fat (g) 20, Trans Fatty Acid (g) 0, Cholesterol (mg) 21, Vitamin D - IU (IU) 0, Calcium (mg) 165, Iron (mg) 5, Magnesium (mg) 130, Potassium (mg) 850, Sodium (mg) 50, Omega 3 Fatty Acid (mg) 3000

Nutrition Facts with Optional Ingredients

Calories (kcal) 800, Protein (g) 21, Carbohydrates (g) 57, Dietary Fiber (g) 10, Soluble Fiber (g) 2, Total Sugars (g) 5, Fat (g) 58, Saturated Fat (g) 7, Mono Fat (g) 29, Poly Fat (g) 20, Trans Fatty Acid (g) 0, Cholesterol (mg) 21, Vitamin D - IU (IU) 0, Calcium (mg) 205, Iron (mg) 7, Magnesium (mg) 160, Potassium (mg) 1100, Sodium (mg) 55, Omega 3 Fatty Acid (g) 3000

Asparagus Leek Frittata (Serves 4)

A frittata is an egg-based dish similar to an omelet but it differs in many ways. First, ingredients are added to the pan and cooked, often on a stove top. The eggs are well whisked until foamy, then poured over the ingredients. This egg mixture is baked in an oven or finished under the broiler. The entire frittata can be brought to the table and cut into radial slices like a pizza.

The frittata is a good example of combining cooking techniques, allowing for less oil and fewer eggs. As such, it is a more convenient way to make interesting eggs dishes that feed the entire family.

The following recipes offer one combination of ingredients. The frittata is a great platform to test new spices and vegetable combinations and offers another way for you to experiment and create in your own kitchen.

4 whole eggs
6 eggs whites
1/2 tsp pepper, fresh ground
1 lb roasted asparagus
2 leeks - white part only, sliced and diced
1 cup mushrooms
1 tbsp parmesan or romano cheese, grated
1/4 cup parsley, fresh chopped
1/2 tsp of dried thyme or marjoram
4 slices tomato, sliced thin

Place asparagus in 400 degree oven for 5-6 minutes. Cut into 1 inch pieces.

Heat a cast iron pan and add oil, leeks, asparagus, mushrooms, and optional spices. Cover and cook until mushrooms are soft.

Place 4 whole eggs and an additional 6 egg whites into a bowl. Add pepper and whisk until foamy. Pour directly into pan over vegetables. Continue to cook on stove top for 3-4 minutes to set egg on bottom, then sprinkle on parmesan cheese and parsley. Place thinly sliced tomatoes on top of eggs at this point. Transfer to the 400 degree oven, remove as the top begins to brown, about 7 minutes. Cut in pizza wedges. At breakfast, serve with fresh fruits. For brunch, lunch, or dinner, serve with a mixed green salad.

Nutrition Facts

Calories (kcal) 185, Protein (g) 15, Carbohydrates (g) 13, Dietary Fiber (g) 3, Soluble Fiber (g) 1, Total Sugars (g) 4, Fat (g) 9, Saturated Fat (g) 2, Mono Fat (g) 3, Poly Fat (g) 1, Trans Fatty Acid (g) 0, Cholesterol (mg) 216, Vitamin D - IU (IU) 0, Calcium (mg) 93, Iron (mg) 3, Magnesium (mg) 36, Potassium (mg) 507, Sodium (mg) 186, Omega 3 Fatty Acid (g) 0

For the Heart of the Eastern Mediterranean

The original study of the heart healthy benefits of the Mediterranean diet focused on the eating patterns of the rural populations, an island in the eastern Mediterranean. It is a style of cooking that begins in Greece and moves around east through through Turkey and then down through Lebanon and Israel. As many cultures have developed around this part of the Mediterranean, the cooking styles and ingredients differ as you make a journey through the region. Some common elements are the extensive use of fresh vegetables, often with a bountiful variety of salads served as a first course. Chick peas, yogurts and spices are important elements in these cuisines.

Greek Barley Salad *(Serves 8)*

Delicious, refreshing and with pungent bursts of flavor, this dish alone makes a great lunch and will help satisfy your appetite throughout the afternoon. It also works as a first course or as a side dish to poached fish or grilled chicken.

4 cups cooked barley pilaf, page 170
1 tsp fresh grated lemon peel
1/2 cup fresh lemon juice
5 tbsp olive oil
2 tbsp pitted kalamata olives, coarsely chopped
1 clove garlic, finely chopped

2 tsp oregano leaves
1/4 tsp ground black pepper
4 pepperoncini peppers, coarsely chopped
2 tsp capers, coarsely chopped
1/4 cup coarsely chopped fresh parsley
1 large red or green pepper, coarsely chopped
1 small cucumber, seeded and coarsely chopped
1 cup cherry tomatoes, halved

Coarsely chop pepper, tomato, cucumber, parsley, pepperoncini, and olives; finely chop capers, lemon peel, onion, and garlic. Combine all other ingredients and then fold into cooled barley pilaf.

Nutrition Facts

Calories (kcal) 295, Protein (g) 5, Carbohydrates (g) 36, Dietary Fiber (g) 8, Soluble Fiber (g) 2, Total Sugars (g) 4, Fat (g) 15, Saturated Fat (g) 2, Mono Fat (g) 11, Poly Fat (g) 2, Trans Fatty Acid (g) 0, Cholesterol (mg) 0, Calcium (mg) 36, Iron (mg) 2, Magnesium (mg) 40, Potassium (mg) 327, Sodium (mg) 198 Omega 3 Fatty Acid (mg) 0

Tabbouleh Revised (Serves 6)

Tabbouleh is a classic Eastern Mediterranean salad that combines bulgur, parsley, lemon, and olive oil. Various vegetables, herbs, and spices can be added to adapt this dish to any season and meal. We again are using the basic barley pilaf for this recipe instead of bulgur to increase the cholesterol-lowering soluble fiber content.

Tabbouleh is one of the few dishes featuring parsley as a central vegetable. Parsley provides significant levels of antioxidants. The mint and red peppers also add to the antioxidant power of this dish. You can also make it in advance and use over a day or two.

3 cups cooked barley pilaf (see recipe on page 170)
3 tbsp extra virgin olive oil
1 large bunch parsley stems removed, finely chopped
Juice of 2 medium lemons

3 tbsp fresh mint, finely chopped
1 medium red pepper
Hot pepper flakes or hot sauce to taste
1/2 medium cucumber, chopped
1 medium tomato, chopped
1/2 sweet red pepper, chopped
6 scallions, finely chopped (or 1/3 sweet onion, finely chopped)
1 clove crushed garlic
Salt to taste

Combine cooled barley pilaf with other ingredients.

Tabbouleh also lends itself to adaptations: Try sweetening it with a 1-2 tablespoons of balsamic vinegar, but reduce the amount of lemon juice to cut the acidic taste. Some people like to add more parsley and mint.

Nutrition Facts

Calories (kcal) 115, Protein (g) 3, Carbohydrates (g) 19, Dietary Fiber (g) 4, Soluble Fiber (g) 1, Total Sugars (g) 2, Fat (g) 4, Saturated Fat (g) 1, Mono Fat (g) 3, Poly Fat (g) 0, Trans Fatty Acid (g) 0, Cholesterol (mg) 0, Calcium (mg) 45, Iron (mg) 2, Magnesium (mg) 26, Potassium (mg) 193, Sodium (mg) 26, Omega 3 Fatty Acid (mg) 0

Kefta

In the Eastern Mediterranean and throughout the Middle East, kefta is made by grinding meat and mixing it with an assortment of spices. Variations of kefta are common street foods -- a more traditional version of fast foods. The spices deliver antioxidants, reducing the inflammatory impact of meats.

Much like ketchup or mustard on burgers, many toppings and sauces can accompany kefta. Typical is a tahini, a delicious sesame based sauce or a Greek tzatziki, a yogurt-based cucumber dip with garlic. Recipes for both follow. Or you can enjoy the same healthy toppings you might put on a burger.

We make kefta heart healthier by blending the meat with black beans. From here, you can take the few additional steps to a meatless black bean burger.

Kefta with Spiced Meat and Beans (Serves 4)

8 ounces ground beef sirloin or ground lamb
8 ounces unsalted cooked black bean, mashed
1/2 cup breadcrumbs
3 egg whites
1/3 cup chopped ,fresh parsley
2 tbsp chopped fresh mint
1 medium onion, finely diced or grated
1 tsp. ground cumin
1/4 tsp. ground turmeric
1 tsp. paprika
1 tsp. ground pepper
1/4 tsp. cinnamon (optional)
1 Tbsp pure olive oil
Salt to taste

Combine all ingredients in a large bowl. Mix well. Let stand 1 hour to blend flavors.

Using about 1/4 mixture for each kebab, mold into a sausage shape around flat metal skewers. Taper ends of sausage shapes to prevent meat from slipping off skewers during cooking. Alternatively, shape into 8 oblong patties. Moistening your hands will help mold the meat mixture. Traditionally kefta are placed over hot coals. Keep at least 4 inches away from the heat source. Brown evenly, and move to part of grill without exposure to direct heat to finish cooking. Total cook time is 8-10 minutes.

Nutrition Facts

Calories (kcal) 210, Protein (g) 18, Carbohydrates (g) 21, Dietary Fiber (g) 7, Soluble Fiber (g) 1, Total Sugars (g) 3, Fat (g) 7, Saturated Fat (g) 2, Mono Fat (g) 4, Poly Fat (g) 1, Trans Fatty Acid (g) 0, Cholesterol (mg) 30, Calcium (mg) 53, Iron (mg) 3, Magnesium (mg) 47, Potassium (mg) 331, Sodium (mg) 97, Omega 3 Fatty Acid (mg) 0

Grilling with the Cooking Cardiologist

Soapstone is the future of the outdoor grill. Yet it has been around for a very long time. Excavations have shown that soapstone has been used as a grilling surface for centuries. Soapstone really could be considered the first non-stick, natural surface.

Consider the following properties that make soapstone utensils ideal for grilling:

- Non-porous and extremely dense
- Non-reactive to acids and chemicals
- Easy to maintain
- Excellent thermal qualities, transferring heat evenly across the surface
- Allows a variety of grilling techniques from baking bread to griddling pancakes to searing meats
- Retains moisture in food
- A natural non-stick surface
- Non-toxic, all natural
- Does not harbor bacteria
- Reduces carcinogens by preventing direct flame contact

While a bit more expensive, soapstone cookware comes in many forms -- roasting pans, pizza pans, griddles, pots of all sizes, and sauté pans, among others. But it's a good investment, both in terms of durability and heart health.

Black Bean Burgers with Kefta Spices *(Serves 4)*

15 ounces cooked black bean
1/2 cup chopped fresh parsley or cilantro
1 small onion
1 tsp. ground cumin
1 tsp. ground paprika (sweet or smoked)
1/2 tsp. ground pepper
1 clove garlic, peeled
1 tsp. pure olive oil
2 eggs, whites only
1/2 cup breadcrumbs, preferably whole wheat
Salt to taste

Place onion and garlic in food processer, process until fine. Add ½ of the black beans and oil. Process until beans are of mashed consistency. Place in a medium mixing bowl. Add remaining beans, spices, bread crumbs, parsley, and egg white. Mix thoroughly, cover and refrigerate for at least an hour. This allows the flavors to blend and allows moisture to be absorbed by the breadcrumbs. If too wet, add more breadcrumbs. Shape into eight small patties, packed firmly. Sauté on medium-high heat until browned on both sides. Lower heat to warm throughout. Serve with the topping of your choice. The bean patties may be frozen in a tightly sealed bag. Browning the burger before freezing will allow the beans to firm for later use on the outdoor grill.

Nutrition Facts

Calories (kcal) 155, Protein (g) 7, Carbohydrates (g) 23, Dietary Fiber (g) 7, Soluble Fiber (g) 0, Total Sugars (g) 3, Fat (g) 4, Saturated Fat (g) 1, Mono Fat (g) 3, Poly Fat (g) 1, Trans Fatty Acid (g) 0, Cholesterol (mg) 0, Calcium (mg) 87, Iron (mg) 3, Magnesium (mg) 55, Potassium (mg) 339, Sodium (mg) 60, Omega 3 Fatty Acid (mg) 0

Greek Tzatziki *(Serves 4)*

2 (8 oz) containers plain lowfat yogurt
2 cucumbers - peeled, seeded and diced
2 tbsp olive oil
1/2 lemon, juiced
Salt and pepper to taste
1 tbsp chopped fresh dill
3 cloves garlic, peeled

In a food processor or blender, combine yogurt, cucumber, olive oil, lemon juice, salt, pepper, dill, and garlic. Process until well-combined. Transfer to a separate dish, cover and refrigerate for at least one hour to allow the flavors to blend.

Nutrition Facts

Calories (kcal) 80, Protein (g) 3, Carbohydrates (g) 7, Dietary Fiber (g) 0, Soluble Fiber (g) 0, Total Sugars (g) 5, Fat (g) 4, Saturated Fat (g) 1, Mono Fat (g) 3, Poly Fat (g) 0, Trans Fatty Acid (g) 0, Cholesterol (mg) 3, Calcium (mg) 115, Iron (mg) 0, Magnesium (mg) 17, Potassium (mg) 227, Sodium (mg) 41, Omega 3 Fatty Acid (mg) 0

Tahini *(Serves 4)*

2 garlic cloves
1/2 cup well-stirred tahini (Middle Eastern sesame paste)
1/2 cup fresh lemon juice
1/4 cup water
1 Tbsp olive oil
2 Tbsp finely chopped fresh cilantro
1/2 cup finely chopped fresh flat-leaf parsley
1/4 teaspoon ground cumin
Salt to taste

Mince garlic, then mash to a paste. Whisk together garlic paste and remaining ingredients until combined well.

Nutrition Facts

Calories (kcal) 220, Protein (g) 5, Carbohydrates (g) 10, Dietary Fiber (g) 2, Soluble Fiber (g) 0, Total Sugars (g) 1, Fat (g) 19, Saturated Fat (g) 3, Mono Fat (g) 9, Poly Fat (g) 7, Trans Fatty Acid (g) 0, Cholesterol (mg) 0, Calcium (mg) 50, Iron (mg) 1, Magnesium (mg) 31, Potassium (mg) 189, Sodium (mg) 12, Omega 3 Fatty Acid (mg) 0

For the Heart
of Morocco

North African cooking is an often-overlooked part of the Mediterranean cuisine. North African cuisine blends savory spices -- turmeric, pepper, saffron, cumin -- with sweeter spices like cinnamon, clover, ginger, and cardamom. Fresh peppermint and parsley also are incorporated in many dishes.

The main meal is typically eaten midday. It usually begins with a collection of salads and is followed by foods made in a tagine, a shallow, circular base pot with a large cone cover (see Figure 9.1). The tagine is designed to prevent any moisture from escaping and returns the liquid to the base where it can intensify the flavors of the dish. The base can be used for serving after the cover is removed.

Figure 9.1. Tagine Used in Cooking

Tagine recipes are cooked slowly so that the finished dish is full of succulence and flavor.

The tagine can be used for a wide variety of meats, vegetables, and fruit dishes. The combination of meats (lamb, beef, or chicken), sweet vegetables (carrots, tomatoes, eggplant) and fruits (lemon, dates, oranges, prunes) is very typical of North African cookery and provides a natural sweetness to many dishes. The sweetness is offset by plenty of spices and cayenne pepper.

> Tagine style cooking epitomizes important heart healthy cooking principles: Emphasis on many high antioxidant spices; the use of lower temperatures; enhancing the flavor of food in its own juices, rather than adding sauces, butters, or creams.

Tagine Recipes

These recipes can be made in a wok or pot with a tight cover. However a tagine is a worthwhile investment, especially if you are serious about heart healthy cooking.

Eggplant Tagine (Serves 4)

1 tbsp teaseed or rice bran oil
1/3 cup chopped garlic
1/3 cup chopped shallots
1 large onion, coarsely chopped
2 red bell peppers, coarsely chopped
1 green bell pepper, coarsely chopped
2 eggplants, washed, unpeeled and sliced into 2-inch slices and then quartered.
3/4 cup no-salt tomato paste
1 cup water or vegetable broth
1 tbsp Moroccan spices (see below)
2 cups cooked garbanzo beans

Moraccan Spice Blend

Here in America, we tend to be very cautious in how we use and mix spices, but remember antioxidant power appears to be intensified by the blending of multiple high micronutrient ingredients. Blending spices also allows you great creativity in the kitchen. Here is a typical blend of spices used in North Africa. It is a starting point for your culinary experimentation.

1 tsp ground cumin
1 tsp ground ginger
3/4 tsp black pepper
1/2 tsp ground cinnamon
1/2 tsp ground coriander
1/2 tsp cayenne
1/2 tsp ground allspice
1/4 tsp ground cloves

Heat oil in tagine on medium heat. Add chopped garlic and shallots. Sauté until fragrant, about 1 minute. Add the onions and peppers, and sauté until the onions are translucent. Season to taste with salt and pepper. Add the eggplant and cook until softened, approximately 5 minutes. Add tomato paste, water or vegetable broth, spices, and beans. Turn down heat to lowest setting and cover with tagine lid. Stir ingredients every 15 minutes. Cook for approximately 50 minutes. Serve with whole wheat couscous or other whole grain.

Nutrition Facts

Calories (kcal) 457, Protein (g) 19, Carbohydrates (g) 85, Dietary Fiber (g) 22, Soluble Fiber (g) 3, Total Sugars (g) 22, Fat (g) 7, Saturated Fat (g) 1, Mono Fat (g) 3, Poly Fat (g) 2, Trans Fatty Acid (g) 0, Cholesterol (mg) 0, Calcium (mg) 145, Iron (mg) 7, Magnesium (mg) 131, Potassium (mg) 1715, Sodium (mg) 73, Omega 3 Fatty Acid (mg) 130

Tagine Salmon (Serves 4)

2 Tbsp teaseed or rice bran oil
4 pods cardamom
1 cinnamon stick
8 whole black peppercorns
2 Tbsp fresh ginger root, grated
1 tsp turmeric
1 tsp cayenne pepper (optional)
4 clove minced garlic
2 Tbsp sweet white wine or vermouth
1 cup fat-free yogurt
1 large white onion, sliced into 1/2-inch thick slices

1 lb salmon fillet, skin removed and cut into 2-inch squares
8 large shrimp, cleaned and deveined with tails
    intact (optional)
Salt to taste

Heat oil in tagine on medium heat. Add cardamom pods, cinnamon, peppercorns, and cloves. When sputtering, add garlic, onions, and ginger. Cook until onions start to brown, watching carefully to avoid burning. Reduce heat to low. Add water, turmeric, garlic, and yogurt. If desired, add optional ingredients - shrimp, and cayenne powder.

Add salmon, cover and simmer 30-45 minutes until cooked. Remove cinnamon sticks and serve with your choice of whole wheat couscous or another whole grain.

Nutrition Facts

Calories (kcal) 324, Protein (g) 32, Carbohydrates (g) 10, Dietary Fiber (g) 1, Soluble Fiber (g) 0, Total Sugars (g) 6, Fat (g) 15, Saturated Fat (g) 3, Mono Fat (g) 6, Poly Fat (g) 5, Trans Fatty Acid (g) 0, Cholesterol (mg) 91, Calcium (mg) 160, Iron (mg) 2, Magnesium (mg) 59, Potassium (mg) 882, Sodium (mg) 124, Omega 3 Fatty Acid (mg) 2300

Tagine Lemon Chicken (*Serves 4*)

2 tbsp teaseed or rice bran oil
1/4 tsp black pepper
1 tsp fresh ginger, grated
1/2 tsp sweet paprika
1 pinch of saffron (optional)
1 tsp cumin
1 tsp turmeric
1/4 tsp ground cinnamon
2 small onions, thinly sliced
2 chicken breasts (4 ounces each, skinned and halved)
2 bay leaves
1/2 cup fresh parsley, chopped
1/2 cup fresh cilantro, chopped
1/4 cup fresh lemon juice
Lemon peel from about 1/2 of lemon, cut into 1-inch long strips

Blend pepper, ginger, sweet paprika, cumin, turmeric, and cinnamon. Coat chicken with this spice blend and place in refrigerator for 3 hours. Heat 2 tablespoons of oil in tagine and add chicken. Lightly brown the chicken. Remove from pan. Add onions, with a small amount of additional oil if needed, and cook until translucent. Reduce heat to medium low, add chicken, a few tablespoons of water, and all other ingredients. Cover tightly and cook until chicken is done, approximately 45-60 minutes. Serve with whole wheat couscous or other whole grain.

Nutrition Facts

Calories (kcal) 203, Protein (g) 24, Carbohydrates (g) 5, Dietary Fiber (g) 1, Soluble Fiber (g) 0, Total Sugars (g) 2, Fat (g) 10, Saturated Fat (g) 2, Mono Fat (g) 4, Poly Fat (g) 2, Trans Fatty Acid (g) 0, Cholesterol (mg) 63, Calcium (mg) 34, Iron (mg) 1, Magnesium (mg) 30, Potassium (mg) 313, Sodium (mg) 61, Omega 3 Fatty Acid (mg) 100

North African Spiced Vegetables (Serves 8)

This recipe complements a tagine dish, grilled fish, or roasted chicken. Also serve cold with a drizzle of balsamic vinegar.

1 large onion, cut in 1/2 inch-thick slices
2 shallots, halved (or quartered if large)
1 large butternut squash, peeled, seeded, and cut into
      1/2 inch cubes
2 large parsnips or carrots
1 large red pepper, cut into 1/2 inch-thick strips
2 sweet potatoes, peeled and cut into cubes
8-10 brussels sprouts, halved
4 tbsp olive oil
2 tsp ground cumin
1 tsp ground coriander
1/2 tsp ground cinnamon
Salt to taste

Preheat oven to 375°F. Toss shallots and onion with 1 tablespoon oil and roast in a shallow pan for 20 minutes. Toss together squash, red peppers, sweet potatoes, brussel sprouts, salt, cumin, coriander, cinnamon, and remaining 3 tbsp oil. Add roasted shallots/onions and spread onto roasting pan or cookie sheet. Roast until vegetables are tender, about 35-45 minutes.

Nutrition Facts

Calories (kcal) 149, Protein (g) 3, Carbohydrates (g) 20, Dietary Fiber (g) 5, Soluble Fiber (g) 1, Total Sugars (g) 6, Fat (g) 8, Saturated Fat (g) 1, Mono Fat (g) 5, Poly Fat (g) 1, Trans Fatty Acid (g) 0, Cholesterol (mg) 0, Calcium (mg) 60, Iron (mg) 1, Magnesium (mg) 39, Potassium (mg) 538, Sodium (mg) 96, Omega 3 Fatty Acid (mg) 40

Other Selected Recipes from the Kardea Kitchen

Green Tea-Poached Halibut with Blueberry Salsa *(Serves 4)*

The recipe is loaded with antioxidants from a number of different sources, including green tea, blueberries, pomegranate juice, and peppers. Poaching with green tea removes fishiness and adds a subtle fresh flavor. It keeps the fish tender and is one of the essential low temperature cooking techniques, submerging food in barely simmering liquid. Poaching occurs at temperatures of 170-180 degrees, well below the boiling point of water.

For the poaching bath:
6 cups prepared green tea (use one teabag for two
cups water)
8 black peppercorns
1/2 tsp fresh ginger root, grated
2 green onions, chopped
4 4-oz halibut fillets

For the salsa:
1/2 cup pomegranate juice (or blueberry juice)
1 tsp balsamic vinegar
1 tsp sugar (optional)
2 cups fresh blueberries, washed and sorted
2 jalapenos, seeded and finely chopped
1 larger red onion, chopped
1 tsp crushed red pepper
Fresh blueberries for garnish

For the salsa: heat pomegranate juice, balsamic vinegar, and sugar. Simmer until soften, approximately 10 minutes. Add the blueberries, jalapenos, red onion, garlic, and red pepper. Simmer until onions softened, approximately 5-7 minutes.

To poach fish, prepare the weak green tea. The green tea flavors will concentrate during poaching. In a medium skillet with 2-inch sides, a saucepan or a fish poacher, add the tea, peppercorns, ginger, and green onions. Bring to a boil. Using a slotted spatula, carefully add the halibut. Each fillet should be fully immersed in the poaching liquid. Bring to boil and remove from heat. Cover. After approximately 10 minutes, carefully remove, placing each fillet over 2-3 tablespoons of salsa. Garnish with fresh blueberries.

Nutrition Facts

Calories (kcal) 318, Protein (g) 19, Carbohydrates (g) 22, Dietary Fiber (g) 3, Soluble Fiber (g) 0, Total Sugars (g) 15, Fat (g) 17, Saturated Fat (g) 3, Mono Fat (g) 10, Poly Fat (g) 2, Trans Fatty Acid (g) 0, Cholesterol (mg) 56, Vitamin D - IU (IU) 572, Calcium (mg) 30, Iron (mg) 2, Magnesium (mg) 48, Potassium (mg) 586, Sodium (mg) 106, Omega 3 Fatty Acid (mg) 1250

Citrus Lime Snapper with
Roasted Corn and Black Beans *(Serves 4)*

This recipe calls for snapper but any firm fish will work. Make extra corn and beans to enjoy as a snack or with lunch.

1 cup corn (2 freshly roasted ears are especially flavorful,
    but frozen also works fine)
1 cup cooked black beans
1/2 cup red onion, diced
1/3 cup fresh cilantro, chopped
2 tbsp rice vinegar
1 jalapeno
1 garlic clove, minced
1 tsp ground chili powder
Salt to taste

Fish marinade:
1/2 cup onion, chopped
1/2 cup fresh lime juice
1 jalapeno, seeded and minced
2 tbsp honey
1 tbsp canola oil
4 4-6 oz red snapper fillet
1/4 tsp pepper
3/4 tsp salt or salt substitute

For salsa, roast the ears of corn, with husks removed, over grill or under a broiler. Turn corn often to prevent excessive browning. If using frozen corn, place in dry sauté pan and roast. Cool. Combine corn, black beans, red onion, cilantro, vinegar, salt, jalapenos, and garlic in a medium bowl. Chill.

For the fish, combine first 5 ingredients and pour over fish. Turn and cover. Let marinate for 20 minutes, turning fish once. Remove. Season with salt and pepper. Place fish in a 350 degree oven, cooking until the fish flakes apart easily. Serve with salsa.

Nutrition Facts

Calories (kcal) 336, Protein (g) 37, Carbohydrates (g) 28, Dietary Fiber (g) 6, Soluble Fiber (g) 1, Total Sugars (g) 12, Fat (g) 9, Saturated Fat (g) 1, Mono Fat (g) 4, Poly Fat (g) 4, Trans Fatty Acid (g) 0, Cholesterol (mg) 52, Calcium (mg) 91, Iron (mg) 2, Magnesium (mg) 102, Potassium (mg) 986, Sodium (mg) 131, Omega 3 Fatty Acid (mg) 800

Chicken in a Balsamic Reduction (*Serves 4*)

A combination of sweet and tart flavors, this dish complements a range of fresh vegetables and whole grains. It is quick and easy to make and only takes about 30 minutes. Make extra; it is great the next day.

1 lb chicken breast or thigh, boneless and skinless
2 cloves garlic
1 tbsp of olive oil
3/4 cup balsamic vinegar
3/4 cup white wine or sweet vermouth
1 tbsp dried porcini mushrooms
Salt and pepper to taste

Place porcini mushroom in wine or vermouth when starting the meal.

Quarter the chicken breasts and slice each into 2 thinner pieces. It can be pounded thinner; or you can purchase thin cut chicken breast at the store. (The thinner the meat, the shorter the cooking time, and the more likely that the taste of the reduction will be absorbed.) Pounding, however, improves the texture of the finished dish.

Crush peeled garlic. Heat a large pan on a medium setting, and then add the olive oil and the garlic. Cook for about a minute, adding the chicken before the garlic begins to brown. Cook on both sides so that the chicken is almost cooked through. Add wine, balsamic vinegar, and porcini mushrooms while the chicken remains in the pan. After about a minute, turn the chicken and cook for another minute. Now remove the chicken from the pan. Bring the remaining liquid to a boil, add ground pepper, and cook for another 4-5 minutes. Pour liquid over chicken. Serve and enjoy.

Sliced and cold, this chicken can also be used in an antipasto. Make a plate with a few olives, some roasted red peppers, a small wedge of aged provolone, a slice of onion, some cut up vegetables, and enjoy with a glass of wine.

Nutrition Facts

Calories (kcal) 268, Protein (g) 27, Carbohydrates (g) 14, Dietary Fiber (g) 0, Soluble Fiber (g) 0, Total Sugars (g) 7, Fat (g) 5, Saturated Fat (g) 1, Mono Fat (g) 3, Poly Fat (g) 1, Trans Fatty Acid (g) 0, Cholesterol (mg) 66, Calcium (mg) 32, Iron (mg) 1, Magnesium (mg) 42, Potassium (mg) 390, Sodium (mg) 89, Omega 3 Fatty Acid (mg) 30

Roast Tuna with Rosemary *(Serves 6-8)*

Carving a holiday roast is traditional with many families. For heart health and cholesterol management, a tuna roast can replace the usual beef or pork tenderloin. While requiring additional preparation, this tuna is a special dish that can help keep you from splurging on unhealthy dishes by providing a delicious and healthy alternative, during holidays and other occasions.

To get the best cut of tuna, you will likely need to go to a fish store or upscale food market. Like any good roast, this tuna not only anchors a festive meal, but also makes great sandwiches the next day.

3-4 lbs tuna (single skinned filet, not steaks)
1/2 fennel bulb, chopped (optional)
2 cloves garlic, chopped (optional)
1 tsp kosher or sea salt (optional)
Marinade
1/2 cup olive oil
1 juice of a medium lemon
1/2 cup white wine preferably one that is not too dry
2 tsp rosemary

Combine ingredients for the marinade and pour over tuna. Let stand in covered bowl outside the refrigerator for about an hour. If you decide to use the fennel, prepare while the tuna is marinating. Beyond its lovely flavor, the fennel serves as a moist bed on which the tuna sits while roasting.

Heat a pan on medium heat and then add about ¼ cup of the marinated, chopped garlic and fennel. Cover and cook until the fennel is tender, stirring occasionally (about 15 minutes). Remove from heat.

Preheat oven to 350 degrees, then heat a large, heavy pan and coat it with olive oil. Brown the tuna on all sides. If using the fennel, remove the tuna and place the sautéed fennel on bottom of pan, then put the tuna on top of fennel. Pour the remaining marinade over the tuna and sprinkle salt. Cover and place in preheated oven. Roast for about 20-25 minutes. Remove from oven. Let cool for about 5-10 minutes. Spoon the gravy from the pan over the tuna, after cutting it into thick medium-rare to medium slices.

Nutrition Facts

Calories (kcal) 318, Protein (g) 40, Carbohydrates (g) 1, Dietary Fiber (g) 0, Soluble Fiber (g) 0, Total Sugars (g) 0, Fat (g) 15, Saturated Fat (g) 3, Mono Fat (g) 8, Poly Fat (g) 3, Trans Fatty Acid (g) 0, Cholesterol (mg) 65, Calcium (mg) 15, Iron (mg) 2, Magnesium (mg) 86, Potassium (mg) 439, Sodium (mg) 357, Omega 3 Fatty Acid (mg) 2000

Zested Scallops with Vermouth and Wilted Greens *(Serves 4)*

Scallops are delicious and useful for a quick evening meal and compared to shrimp, have much less cholesterol, only about 35mg per serving. Raw scallops also freeze well, retaining both sweetness and tenderness. One serving delivers about 400mg of Omega-3s.

12 large raw sea scallops
1/2 cup dry vermouth
1/2 tsp fennel seed, chopped fine
2 tsp lemon zest, chopped coarse
1 tbsp olive oil
1/4 cup fresh parsley, chopped coarse

On a medium setting, heat a pan large enough to place all the scallops on the bottom with some space between each. When hot, coat bottom with olive oil. Add vermouth and scallops. Cover for 3 minutes. Remove from heat and add lemon zest. Cover for another minute. Add fresh parsley and serve.

Wash spinach carefully, making sure to remove all dirt. To clean, fill a pot with water and drop leaves in. The heavier dirt particles will fall to the bottom while the leaves float. Remove the spinach, place in a colander, rinse, and drain.

Heat a large frying pan on a medium-low to medium heat. Add 1½ tbsp of olive oil. When oil is hot, add garlic and then quickly add the spinach to the pan. Cover tightly. After the spinach has wilted, stir to assure that oil and garlic lightly coat all the leaves. Remove from pan and use a bed to serve the scallops.

If you have any left over, serve cold on a crusty roll with a slice of tomato, a few diced capers, a drizzle of olive oil, and bit of Dijon mustard.

Nutrition Facts

Calories (kcal) 233, Protein (g) 22, Carbohydrates (g) 17, Dietary Fiber (g) 5, Soluble Fiber (g) 0, Total Sugars (g) 0, Fat (g) 8, Saturated Fat (g) 1, Mono Fat (g) 5, Poly Fat (g) 1, Trans Fatty Acid (g) 0, Cholesterol (mg) 37, Calcium (mg) 113, Iron (mg) 4, Magnesium (mg) 66, Potassium (mg) 395, Sodium (mg) 365, Omega 3 Fatty Acid (mg) 220

Mediterranean Tuna Salad

Here is a heart healthier way to make a delicious tuna salad. It is quick, easy and delicious.

1 5 ounce can tuna, water packed (or water-packed sardines)
2 cups artichoke hearts, water packed
1/2 cup scallions, chopped
1 red or green pepper, chopped
2 cups cherry tomatoes, halved
2 cups leaf lettuce, chopped
1 cup fresh spinach, chopped
1 medium cucumber, chopped
1 cup chick peas
3 tbsp extra virgin olive oil
4 tbsp balsamic vinegar

Optional Ingredients
1 tablespoon capers
1/2 cup olives

Combine all ingredients in a bowl. Serve as a lunch or as a component of a first course antipasti. Garnish with a lemon wedge. This also makes for a great sandwich. Try replacing the tuna wth sardines. This recipe is a great way to introduce sardines into the meal rotation. Sardines have an advantage over tuna in that they provide higher levels of Omega-3s and come from a more sustainable fish population.

Nutritional Facts

Calories (kcal) 305, Protein (g) 18, Carbohydrates (g) 34, Dietary Fiber (g) 14, Soluble Fiber (g) 3, Total Sugars (g) 10, Fat (g) 12, Saturated Fat (g) 2, Mono Fat (g) 8, Poly Fat (g) 2, Cholesterol (mg) 11, Calcium (mg) 100, Iron (mg) 4, Magnesium (mg) 101, Potassium (mg) 976, Sodium (mg) 90

Balancing Acts

Great meals bring a range of tastes and textures to the table and include multiple dishes. For the everyday dinner, you may be looking at only two or three dishes. For holidays and celebrations, there may be many more. Through multiple dishes, you also have a greater opportunity to strike a smart balance between mostly healthy ingredients and others that are simply delicious.

The healthiest meals also bring a range of nutrients to the table — not just the right carbohydrates and adequate levels of the right protein and the healthier fats, but also vitamins, minerals, and other nutrients that can serve to control the inflammatory process.

While often underused, beans, greens, and whole grains provide taste, texture, and healthy balance to meals. Here are some quick tips to help you incorporate them into your daily menu.

Beans

Beans deliver a tremendous mix of proteins, cholesterol-lowering fibers, potassium, and other micronutrients. Black and dark red beans are also good sources of antioxidants. Beans blend well with any number of spices, another source of high antioxidant compounds. Beans are inexpensive, and when properly prepared — in soups and chilis, in spreads and hummus, as salads and "baked," or with rice, pastas, or other whole grains — can find a place at any meal or in any course. Spiced roasted beans also make a great snack. Bean dishes can be made with meat, with dairy, or for vegans, satisfying the taste and texture cravings of almost any eater.

The internet has countless bean recipes. Assuming that the beans are ready for use, many of these recipes can be made quickly. You certainly can purchase precooked canned beans, although they should be low in sodium. Starting with dried beans, however, has advantages. They typically are more flavorful and have a better texture. However, dried beans take time to cook.

Standard recipes call for the dried beans to be soaked in water at room temperature. The larger the bean, the longer they need to soak. Many recipes simply recommend that the beans get soaked overnight. The longer they soak, the shorter time they'll need to cook. But soaking them too long can cause them to ferment and affect the flavor.

Dried beans will expand as they are soaked and cook. Keep this in mind when reading a recipe. Does it call for dried or cooked beans? A rule of thumb: one cup of dried beans will yield 3 cups of cooked beans.

Some recipes also recommend that you accelerate the soaking process by bringing the beans to a boil and then letting them sit covered for another 1-2 hours. But unlike soaking alone, adding heat will result in nutrients like antioxidants leaching into the surrounding water. Since soaking water is typically discarded, the beans will lose some of their nutritive value.

After soaking, drain the beans and add fresh water to the cooking pot. The beans are now ready for cooking. Depending on what you are making, the beans may be cooked through before being added into other dishes. For soups and casseroles, ingredients are added before the beans are fully cooked.

Tips from the Cooking Cardiologist: Beans and Pressure Cookers

Living in Denver, at high altitude, I face some cooking challenges. Water will boil at 212°F at sea level, but will reach only a temperature of 202°F at 5,000 feet and 199°F at 7,000 feet. In Leadville (highest city in America at 10,000 feet), water will boil at 195°F. A pressure cooker will "even the score" for altitude and bring food to higher temperatures.

Pressure cooking equipment has greatly improved since your grandmother's day. New versions of pressure cookers have backup safety measures to prevent an eruption in your kitchen, which can result in a huge mess. A pressure cooker will cook items up to three times faster, at lightning speed for beans, rice, and legumes.

Greens

Americans moving to heart healthier eating often enjoy salad, steamed broccoli, and peas. Missing from many diets are the green leafy vegetables like spinach, kale, chard, collards, and others that deliver high levels of useful micronutrients. Often when these vegetables are eaten, they are cooked in a fair amount of oil, sharply increasing their caloric levels.

One way to make greens healthy and delicious is a water sauté. Put just enough oil in a larger pan to allow your choice of herbs and spices to cook and sweeten at a low temperature. You can then add a liquid, some combination of water, wine, vinegar, vermouth, or tomato or fruit juices.

You pick the combination; try different options. If you are feeling especially adventurous, add some other spices like a mild curry or chipotle hot sauce. Then put in the greens, toss, and cover, letting them cook until they are tender. Spinach and chard cook quickly. Kale and collards take longer.

Whole Grain Cookery

Americans enjoy whole grains in breakfast cereals, sandwich breads, and perhaps pasta or brown rice. Many other whole grains can add excellent taste, texture, and balance to just about every meal.

The challenge is that whole grains can take a long time to cook, and are thus difficult to bring into our everyday eating patterns. No doubt one of the reasons our ancestors milled and processed grains was to accelerate the cooking the process.

But you can adapt whole grain cooking to your lifestyle, hectic or not. Whole grains can be cooked on the stove, in a countertop steamer or rice cooker; or in a pressure cooker, microwave, or crock pot. Rice cookers include timers to start the process and use a sensor to determine when the liquid has been absorbed by the grains.

Desserts:
Small Celebrations
to the Healthy Meal

In the world of delicious and harmful, desserts often are the most tempting. Some of the greatest culinary artistry comes from pastry chefs and chocolatiers. Ice creams and custards, fine pastries and pies, cakes and cookies, chocolate, and other confections can delight, but deliver few nutrients that help, lots of calories, and many nutrients that harm.

Certainly, fruit and some nuts can be a healthy exception. You can enjoy sorbet or perhaps a dark chocolate truffle with nuts and berries.

Most cookbooks end with dessert recipes. We stop short of that and simply reiterate our philosophy about desserts. The key is to remember that delicious desserts are the exclamation point to an otherwise healthy meal. Keep the portion small; they should never be considered another course. Eat them slowly, relish the flavors, textures, and sensations. Avoid having them in pantry shelves or freezers. Buy only the amount you need to enjoy at the coming meal.

ENDNOTES

1   T. Colin Campbell and Thomas M Campbell, *The China Study: Startling Implications for Diet, Weight Loss and Long-Term Health* (Dallas: Benbella, 2006).

2   Dean Ornish, MD, *Reversing Heart Disease* (New York: Random House, 1996).

3   Caldwell B. Esselstyn, Jr., MD, *Prevent and Reverse Heart Disease* (New York: Avery, 2007).

4   Joel Fuhrman, *Cholesterol Protection for Life: Lower Your Cholesterol Safely and Permanently* (Fleming, NJ: Gift of Health Press, 2007).

5   Robert Pritikin, MD, *The Pritikin Program: The Premier Health and Fitness Program for the '90s* (New York: Simon and Schuster 1990).

6   *Your Guide to Lowering Cholesterol with Therapeutic Lifestyle Changes* (Washington, DC: National Institute of Heart, Lung and Blood Institute, National Institutes of Health, 2006).

7   *The Seventh Report of the Joint National Committee on Prevention, Detection and Treatment of High Blood Pressure*, (Washington, DC: U.S. Department of Health and Human Services, National Institutes of Health, National Heart, Lung, and Blood Institute, August 2004), 25.

8   The Florida Department of Citrus, State of Florida, 2008.

9   E. Ford, M.D. et al *"Trends in the Prevalence of Low Risk Factor Burden for Cardiovascular Disease Among U.S. Adults"* Circulation (2009) 120: 1165-1167.

10   *Lowering Your Blood Pressure with DASH*, NIH Publication No. 06-4082 (Washington, DC: U.S. Department of Health and Human Services National Institutes of Health National Heart, Lung, and Blood Institute, April, 2006).

11   SR Daniels, F Greer, et al, *"Lipid Screening and Cardiovascular Health,"* Childhood Pediatrics 122, no. 1 (July 2008)198-208.

12   Ibid

13   *Detection, Evaluation and Treatment of High Blood Cholesterol in Adults: Third Report of the National Cholesterol Education Program Expert Panel* (National Institute of Heart, Lung and Blood Institute, National Institutes of Health 2002).

14   J Stephens et al, *"The Biological Relevance and Measurement of Plasma Markers of Oxidative Stress,"* Diabetes and Cardiovascular Disease Atherosclerosis 202 (2009) 321-9.

15   Ibid

16   J O'Keefe et al, *"Dietary Strategies for Improving Post-Prandial Glucose, Lipids, Inflammation, and Cardiovascular Health,"* Journal of the American College of Cardiology 51, iss. 3 (22 January 2008) 249-55.

17   C Fryar et al *Hypertension, High Serum Total Cholesterol, and Diabetes: Racial and Ethnic Prevalence Differences in U.S. Adults* (Hyattsville, MD: National Center for Health Statistics,1999-2006)

18   *"Prehypertension, Prediabetes Predict Heart Risk Medicine,"* www.medicinenet.com, May 3, 2010.

19   Ibid

20   *Health, United States, 2009 in Brief* Centers for Disease Control, United States Department of Health and Human Service, (2009)

21   *"Heart Disease and Stroke Prevention: Addressing the Nation's Leading Killers At A Glance"* Center for Disease Control and Prevention,http://www.cdc.gov/chronicdisease/resources/publications/AAG/dhdsp.htm, 2010.

22   *Health, United States, 2009 in Brief* Centers for Disease Control, United States Department of Health and Human Service, (2009)

23   L Tanner *"Blood Pressure Goal Met, But Too Many Still Have"* The Associated Press – Online, May 25, 2010.

24   S Liu, *"A Prospective Study of Dietary Glycemic Load, Carbohydrate Intake, and Risk of Coronary Heart Disease in US Women,"* American Journal of Clinical Nutrition, 71, no. 6 (June 2000) 1455-61.

25   O'Keefe et al, 249-55.

26   Liu, 1455-61.

27   Ibid

28   J Keogh *"Flow-Mediated Dilatation Is Impaired by a High–Saturated Fat Diet but Not by a High-Carbohydrate Diet"* Arteriosclerosis, Thrombosis, and Vascular Biology. (2005)25:1274.

29   Ibid

30   Arthur Agatston, MD, *The South Beach Diet: The Delicious, Doctor-Designed, Foolproof Plan for Fast and Healty Weight Loss* (New York: St Martin's, 2003).

31   Arthur Agatston, MD, *The South Beach Heart Program: The 4-Step Plan That Can Save Your Life* (New York, Rodale, 2007).

32   D Mazaffarian, MD et al, *"Trans Fatty Acids and Cardiovascular Disease,"* The New England Journal of Medicine 354 (2006)1601-13

33   Ibid

34   N de Roos, et al, *"Replacement of Dietary Saturated Fatty Acids by Trans Fatty Acids Lowers Serum HDL Cholesterol and Impairs Endothelial Function in Healthy Men and Women,"* Arteriosclerosis, Thrombosis, and Vascular Biology 21 (2001)1233.

35   E Lopez-Garcia, et al, *"Major Dietary Patterns Are Related to Plasma Concentrations of Markers of Inflammation and Endothelial Dysfunction, American Journal of Clinical Nutrition"* American Journal of Clinical Nutrition 80 (2004) 1029-35.

36   Ibid

37   Ibid

38   TT Fung et al, *"Association between Dietary Patterns and Plasma Biomarkers of Obesity and Cardiovascular Disease Risk,"* American Journal of Clinical Nutrition 73 (2001) 61-67.

39   DE King et al, *"Relation of Dietary Fat and Fiber to Elevation of C-reactive Protein,"* American Journal of Cardiology 9 (2003) 1335-39.

40   S Nicholls, PhD. et al *"Consumption of Saturated Fat Impairs the Anti-Inflammatory Properties of High-Density Lipoproteins and Endothelial Function,"* Journal of the American College of Cardiology 48, issue 4 (15 August 2006) 715-720.

41   F Fuentes et al, *"Mediterranean and Lowfat Diets Improve Endothelial Function in Hypercholesterolemic Men,"* Annals of Internal Medicine 134, no. 12 (June 19, 2001) 1115-19.

42   DJ Baer et al, *"Dietary Fatty Acids Affect Plasma Markers of Inflammation in Healthy Men Fed Controlled Diets: A Randomized Crossover Study,"* American Journal of Clinical Nutrition 79 (2004) 969-973.

43   M Esposito et al, *"Effects of a Mediterranean-Style Diet on the Endothelial Dysfunction and Markers of Vascular Inflammation in Metabolic Syndrome,"* Journal of the American Medical Association 292 (2004) 1440-46.

44   W Harris et al, *"Omega-6 Fatty Acids and Risk for Cardiovascular Disease: A Science Advisory From the American Heart Association Nutrition Subcommittee of the Council on Nutrition, Physical Activity, and Metabolism; Council on Cardiovascular Nursing; and Council on Epidemiology and Prevention,"* Circulation 119 (2009) 902-7.

45   K Westerterp, *"Diet Induced Therrmogenesis,"* Nutrition and Metabolism 1 (2004)5.

46   C Johnston, *"Postprandial Thermogenesis Is Increased 100% on a High-Protein, Low-Fat Diet versus a High-Carbohydrate, Lowfat Diet in Healthy, Young Women,"* Journal of the American College of Nutrition, 21, no. 1 (2002) 55-61.

47   D Jenkins et al, *"The Effect of a Plant-Based Low-Carbohydrate ('Eco-Atkins') Diet on Body Weight and Blood Lipid Concentrations in Hyperlipidemic Subjects,"* Archives of Internal Medicine 169, no. 11 (June 2009),[1046-1054].

48   L Appel, *"Dietary Approaches to Prevent and Treat Hypertension: A Scientific Statement From the American Heart Association,"* 47 (2006) 296-308.

49   LD Youngman et al, *"Protein Oxidation Associated with Aging Is Reduced By Dietary Restriction of Protein or Calories,"* Proceedings of the National Academy of Science 89, no. 19 (October 1, 1992) 9112-16.

50   A Sanz et al, *"Carbohydrate restriction Does Not Change Mitochondrial Free Radical Generation and Oxidative DNA Damage,"* Journal of Bioenergetics and Biomembranes 38, nos. 5-6 (December, 2006).

51   A Sanz et al, *"Protein Restriction Without Strong Caloric Restriction Decreases Mitochondrial Oxygen Radical Production and Oxidative DNA Damage in Rat Liver,"* Journal of Bioenergetics and Biomembranes 36 (December 2004)

52   E. Westman, M.D. et al *The New Atkins For Your* , (New York: Fireside, 2010).

53   TP Erlinger and LJ Appel, *"Dietary Patterns and Coronary Heart Disease Risk,"* in Coronary Heart Disease Epidemiology (Oxford, UK: Oxford University Press, 2005).

54   A Keyes, et al *"Coronary Heart Disease in Seven Countries,"* Circulation 41 (April 1970)

55   WC Willett , et al, *"Mediterranean Diet Pyramid: A Cultural Model vor Healthy Eating,"* American Journal of Clinical Nutrition 61, no. 6 (June 1, 1995).1402S–6S.

56   A Keys et al., *"The Diet and 15-Year Death Rate in the Seven Countries Study,"* American Journal of Epidemiology 124, no. 6 (December 1986) 903–15.

57   Campbell and Campbell.

58   Ibid

59   Ibid

60   WC Cockerham et al, *"Okinawa: An Exception to the Social Gradient of Life Expectancy in Japan,"* Asia Pacific Journal of Clinical Nutrition 10 (2001) 154-8.

61   HO Bang, et al , *"The Composition of the Eskimo Food in North Western Greenland,"* American Journal of Clinical Nutrition 33, no. 12 (December 1980) 2657-61.

62   JC Hansen, et al , *"Fatty Acids and Antioxidants in the Inuit Diet. Their Role in Ischemic Heart Disease (IHD) and Possible Interactions With Other Dietary Factors. A Review,"* Arctic Medical Research 53, no 1 (Jan 1994)4-17.

63   Esselstyn.

64   Fuhrman and Ornish.

65   American Heart Association, NIH.

66   Global Prevalence of Vitamin A Deficiency in Populations At Risk 1995-2005 (Geneva, Switzerland: World Health Organization, 2009).

67   M.Kata, PhD, ET AL *"Efficacy and Safety of Plant Stanols and Sterols in the Management of Blood Cholesterol Levels"* Mayo Clinic Proceedings 2003; 78: pages 965-978.

68   A Basu, *"Dietary Factors That Promote or Retard Inflammation Arteriosclerosis, Thrombosis and Vascular Biology,"* 26 (2006) 995-1001.

69   P Kris-Etherton, PhD, RD, et a l *"AHA Scientific Statement: Fish Consumption, Fish Oil, Omega-3 Fatty Acids, and Cardiovascular Disease"* Circulation. 2002;106:2747.

70   Lichtenstein et al. *"Diet and Lifestyle Recommendations Revision*

2006, *A Scientific Statement from the American Heart Association Nutrition Committee,*" circular, June 2006.

71   A Simopoulous, *"The Importance of the Omega-6/Omega-3 Fatty Acid Ratio in Cardiovascular a Disease and Other Chronic Diseases,"* Experimental Biology and Medicine 233 (2008) 674-88.

72   Ibid

73   S Wang et al, *"Reduction in Dietary Omega-6 Polyunsaturated Fatty Acids: Eicosapentaenoic Acid Plus Docosahexaenoic Acid Ratio Minimizes Atherosclerotic Lesion Formation and Inflammatory Response in LDL Receptor Null Mouse,"* Atherosclerosis 204 (1 May 2009)147-55.

74   W Harris et al, *"Omega-6 Fatty Acids and Risk for Cardiovascular Disease,"* Circulation 119 (February 2009) 902-7.

75   A Goldberg, et al, *"Multiple-Dose Efficacy and Safety of an Extended-Release Form of Niacin in the Management of Hyperlipidemia,"* The American Journal of Cardiology 85 (May 1, 2000) 1100-5.

76   76 J Wink, M.D. et al *"Effect of Very Low Dose Niacin on High Density Lipoprotein in Patients Undergoing Long Term Statin Therapy"* American Heart Journal, (March 2002) Volume 143. Number 3

77   Goldberg, 1102

78   Red Yeast Rice Supplement Review Consumer Labs, (July 2008)

79   J Vogel, et al, *"Integrating Complementary Medicine into Cardiovascular Medicine: A Report of the American College of Cardiology Foundation,"* Journal of the American College of Cardiology 46, no. 1 (2005)

80   C Strey et al, *"Endothelium-Ameliorating Effects of Statin Therapy and Coenzyme Q10 Reductions in Chronic Heart Failure,"* Atherosclerosis 179, issue 1 (March 2005) 201-6.

81   J Nawarskas, *"HMG-CoA Reductase Inhibitors and Coenzyme Q10,"* Cardiology in Review 13, issue 2 (March/April 2005) 76-9.

82   G Caso et al, *"Effect of Coenzyme Q10 on Myopathic Symptoms in Patients Treated With Statins,"* The American Journal of Cardiology 99, issue 10 (2007) 1409-12.

83   LJ Appel et al. *"A Clinical Trial of the Effects of Dietary Patterns On Blood Pressure,"* New England Journal of Medicine 336 (1997)1117-24.

84   *Dietary Reference Intakes for Water, Potassium, Sodium, Chloride, and Sulfate, National Academy of Sciences.* Institute of Medicine, Food and Nutrition Board, 2004.

85   D Naismith, *"The Effect of Low-Dose Potassium Supplementation on Blood Pressure in Apparently Healthy Volunteers,"* British Journal of Nutrition 90 (2003) 53-60.

86   KT Khaw et al, *"Dietary Potassium and Stroke-Associated Mortality. A 12-Year Prospective Population Study,"* New England Journal of Medicine 316, no. 5

(January 29, 1987) 235-240.

87   H Adrogue et al, *"Sodium and Potassium in the Pathogenesis of Hypertension,"* New England Journal of Medicine 356(May 10, 2007) 1966-1978.

88   PK Whelton , J He, LJ Appel , et al. *"Primary Prevention of Hypertension: Clinical and Public Health Advisory from the National High Blood Pressure Education Program,"* Journal of the American Medical Association 288 (2002) 1882-88.

89   *Dietary Reference Intakes for Water, Potassium, Sodium, Chloride, and Sulfate* National Academy of Sciences, Institute of Medicine, Food and Nutrition Board, 2004.

90   Ibid

91   JD Keaney, et al, *"Antioxidant Protection of Low-Density Lipoprotein and Its Role in the Prevention of Atherosclerotic Vascular Disease."* Natural Antioxidants in Human Health and Disease, edited by B Frei (San Diego: Academic Press, 1994) 303-52.

92   D Pratico, *"Antioxidants and Endothelium Protection,"* Atherosclerosis (2 August 2005) 181: 215-24.

93   S Steinhubl *"Why Have Antioxidants Failed in Clinical Trials?"* American Journal of Cardiology (May 22 , 2008)Volume 101, Issue 10, Supplement, S14-S19.

94   Ibid

95   JR Prior et al, *"Plasma Antioxidant Capacity Changes Following a Meal as a Measure of the Ability of a Food to Alter In Vivo,"* Antioxidant Status Journal 26, no. 2 (2007)170-81.

96   Ibid

97   Ibid

98   Ibid

99   F Brighenti et al, *"Total Antioxidant Capacity of the Diet Is Inversely and Independently Related to Plasma Concentration of High-Sensitivity C-Reactive Protein in Adult Italian Subjects,"* British Journal of Nutrition 93 (2005) 619-25.

100 OK Chun et al, *"Serum C-Reactive Protein Concentrations Are Inversely Associated with Dietary Flavonoid Intake in U.S. Adults,"* Journal of Nutrition, 138 (April 2008) 753-60.

101 S Shobana, *"Antioxidant Activity of Selected Indian Spices,"* Prostaglandins, Leukotrienes and Essential Fatty Acids 62, issue 2 (February 2000) 107-10.

102 Deborah Kotz, *"Time in the Sun: How Much Is Needed for Vitamin D?"* US News and World Report, June 23, 2008.

103 J Lappe *"Vitamin D and calcium supplementation reduces cancer risk: results of a randomized trial"* American Journal of Clinical Nutrition, Vol. 85, No. 6 (June 2007) 1586-1591.

104   J Witte *"Depression Is Associated With Decreased 25-Hydroxyvitamin D and Increased Parathyroid Hormone Levels in Older Adults"* Archives of General Psychiatry Vol 65, No 5 (2008)508-512.

105   M Holick *"Vitamin D: importance in the prevention of cancers, type 1 diabetes, heart disease, and osteoporosis"* American Journal of Clinical Nutrition Vol. 79, No. 3 (March 2004) 362-371.

106   R Chernoff and PM Suter, eds *"Ageing: biology and nutrition,"* 11, issue 1 (January 2008) 7-12.

107   Brian Wansink, Mindless Eating (New York: Bantam, 2006) 25.

108   Nanci Hellmich, *"Survey: Restaurants Dishing Out Extra-Large Portions,"* USA Today, October 21, 2006.

109   Ibid

110   J O'Keefe et al, *"Dietary Strategies for Improving Post-Prandial Glucose, Lipids, and More: Post-Prandial Hyperlipemia,"* Journal of the American College of Cardiology 51, no. 3 (2008).

111   W Tsai et al, *"Effects of Oxidative Stress on Endothelial Function after a High-Fat Meal,"* Clinical Science 106 (2004)315-19.

112   K Node, et al, *"Postprandial Hyperglycemia as an Etiological Factor in Vascular Failure,"* Cardiovascular Diabetology 8 (2009) 23.

113   T Kolettis, *"Afternoon Nap, Meal Ingestion and Circadian Variation of Acute Myocardial Infarction,"* International Journal of Cardiology 123, issue 3, (24 January 2008) 338-40.

114   A Margioris, *"Fatty Acids and Postprandial Inflammation: Current Opinion,"* Clinical Nutrition and Metabolic Care 12 (2009) 129-137.

115   S Renaud , RM de Lorgeril, *"Wine, Alcohol, Platelets, and the French Paradox for Coronary Heart Disease,"* Lancet 339, no 8808 (1992 Jun 20) 1523-6.

116   RM de Longeril, et al, *"Mediterranean Alpha-Linolenic Acid-rich Diet in Secondary Prevention of Coronary Heart Disease,"* Lancet (March 1995)1454-9.

117   P Kris-Etherton, et al, *"Fish Consumption, Fish Oil, Omega-3 Fatty Acids, and Cardiovascular Diseases,"* Circulation.

118   F Centritto et al, *"Dietary patterns, Cardiovascular Risk Factors And C-Reactive Protein In a Healthy Italian Population,"* Nutrition, Metabolism and Cardiovascular Diseases 10, no. 19 (December 2009)697-706.

119   L Azadbakht, A Esmaillzadeh, *"Red Meat Intake Is Associated with Metabolic Syndrome and the Plasma C-Reactive Protein Concentration in Women,"* Journal of Nutrition, 139, no. 2 (February 2009) 335-39.

120   L Zhaoping, et al, *"Antioxidant-Rich Spice Added to Hamburger Meat During Cooking Results in Reduced Meat, Plasma, and Urine Malondialdehyde,"* American Journal of Clinical Nutrition 91, no. 5 (May 2010) 1180-84.

121   S. Shobana, *"Antioxidant Activity of Selected Indian Spices,"* Prostaglandins,

Leukotrienes and Essential Fatty Acids 62, issue 2 (February 2000) 107-10.

122   Hodgson, J M et al, *"Acute Effects of Tea in Fasting and Postprandial Vascular Function and Blood Pressure in Humans,"* Journal of Hypertension 23, issue 1 (January 2005) 47-54.

123   E Levitan, *"Association Between Consumption of Beer, Wine, and Liquor and Plasma Concentration of High-Sensitivity C-Reactive Protein in Women Aged 39 to 89 Years"* The American Journal of Cardiology 96, issue 1, (July 1, 2005) 83-88.

124   C Williams, *"Nutritional Quality of Organic Food: Shades of Grey or Shades of Green?"* Proceedings of the Nutrition Society 61 (2002) 19-24.

125   F Magkos, *"Buying More Safety or Just Peace of Mind? A Critical Review of the Literature"* Critical Reviews in Food Science and Nutrition 46, no. 1 (2006) 23-56.

126   S Wang, et al, *"Antioxidant Activity in Fruits and Leaves of Blackberry, Raspberry, and Strawberry Varies with Cultivar and Developmental Stage,"* Journal of Agriculture and Food Chemistry 48, no. 2 (2000) 140-6.

127   AM Connor et al, *"Changes in Fruit Antioxidant Activity among Blueberry Cultivars during Cold-Temperature Storage,"* Journal of Agriculture and Food Chemistry 50, no. 4 (2002) 893-8.

128   A Raffo, *"Nutritional Value of Cherry Tomatoes (Lycopersicon esculentum Cv. Naomi F1) Harvested at Different Ripening Stages,"* Journal of Agriculture and Food Chemistry 50, issue 22 (2002), 6550–56.

129   A Marin, et al *"Characterization and Quantitation of Antioxidant Constituents of Sweet Pepper (Capsicum annuum L.)"* Journal of Agriculture and Food Chemistry 52 (12), (2004) 3861–3869.

130   A Addie, *"Activity and Concentration of Polyphenolic Antioxidants in Apple: Effect of Cultivar, Harvest Year, and Storage Conditions,"* Journal of Agriculture and Food Chemistry 49, issue 8 (2001) 3606-13.

131   D O'Beirne et al, *"Fate of Antioxidants in Fresh-Cut Produce: Processing and Storage Conditions to Maximize Asia Pacific,"* Symposium on Assuring Quality and Safety of Agri-Foods International Society for Horticulture Science, [location of symposium?] , 2008.

132   D Zhang, *"Antioxidant Activity and Total Phenolics in Post-Harvest Iceberg Lettuce,"* XXVI International Horticultural Congress: Issues and Advances in Postharvest Horticulture, [location of Congress?], 2002.

133   C Kevers, et al *"Evolution of Antioxidant Capacity During Storage of Selected Fruits & Vegetables"* Journal of Agriculture and Food Chemistry 55 (21) (2007) 8596-8603.

134   I Birlouez-Aragon et al, *"A Diet Based on High-Heat-Treated Foods Promotes Risk Factors for Diabetes Mellitus And Cardiovascular Diseases,"* American Journal of Clinical Nutrition 91, no. 5 (May 2010) 1220-26.

135 *"Heat Generated Food Toxicants: Identification, Characterisation and Risk Minimisation (HEATOX)"* European Commission of Food Quality and Safety (2003).

136 E Linos, et al, *"Red Meat Consumption during Adolescence among Premenopausal Women and Risk of Breast Cancer,"* Cancer Epidemiology, Biomarkers and Prevention 17, no. 8 (2008) 2146–51.

137 D Tang, et al, *"Grilled Meat Consumption and PhIP-DNA Adducts in Prostate Carcinogenesis,"* Biomarkers and Prevention 16, no 4 (2007) 803–8.

138 M Cotterchio, et al, *"Red Meat Intake, Doneness, Polymorphisms in Genes that Encode Carcinogen-Metabolizing Enzymes, and ColorectalCancer Risk,"* Biomarkers and Prevention 17, no 11 (2008) 3098–107.

139 R Murphy et al, *"Cooking Does Not Decrease Hydrophillic Antioxidant Capacity of Wild Blueberries,"* International Journal of Food Sciences and Nutrition 60, supplement 2 (February 2009) 88-98.

140 S Gorinstein, et al *"Raw and boiled garlic enhances plasma antioxidant activity and improves plasma lipid metabolism in cholesterol-fed rats"* Life Sciences 78 (6) (2006) 655-663.

141 K Hunter et al, *"The Antioxidant Activity and Composition of Fresh, Frozen, Jarred and Canned Vegetables,"* Innovative Food Science & Emerging Technologies 3, issue 4 (December 2002) 399-406.

142 J Monreal et al, *"Influence of Cooking Methods on Antioxidant Activity of Vegetables,"* Journal of Food Science, 74, no. 3 (2009) H97.

143 Ibid

144 Ibid

145 0 M Chohan. et al *"Determinants of the Antioxidant Capacity of Culinary Herbs Subject to Various Cooking Methods"* Plant Foods Human Nutrition Volume 3, Number 2 (June 2008)

146 J Kaloustian *"Effect of Wate Cooking on Free Sterol Levels in Beans & Vegetables"* Food Chemistry Volume 107, (April 2008) pp 1379-1386.

147 M Naruszewicz, *"Chronic Intake of Potato Chips in Humans Increases the Production of Reactive Oxygen Radicals By Leukocytes and Increases Plasma C-Reactive Protein: A Pilot Study,"* American Journal of Clinical Nutrition 89, no. 3 (March 2009) 773-7.

INDEX

Note: *f* represents a figure.

About the Authors

DR. RICHARD COLLINS, MD
CARDIOLOGIST

Over a long career as a cardiologist, Mayo Clinic-trained Dr. Richard Collins saw remarkable improvements in his profession's ability to save lives. A continuous flow of advances in drugs and medical procedures allowed all cardiologists to improve their patients' odds of survival and recovery after a heart attack.

A turning point in his career came when he met a patient who, then in his mid-sixties, just had his third bypass operation. Another operation was not an option. In the search for an alternative, the patient traveled to Sausalito, CA to undergo an innovative treatment approach under Dr. Dean Ornish at the Preventative Medicine and Research Institute. The program had four components: a low-fat vegetarian diet, stress management/yoga, support group processing and exercise. All components were administered simultaneously. The results were astonishing. The patient lived until he was 81 without any additional heart procedures.

Dr. Collins brought the Ornish approach into his own practice. "The impact was impressive, but its success required a tremendous amount of restraint," recalls Dr. Collins. "Many people simply could or would not stay on this program for an extended period. Certainly, those at very high risk proved motivated, but for many others, the dietary disciplines proved too challenging."

Today, Dr. Collins is the director of wellness at a leading cardiology group in the Denver, CO area. This is a unique practice. The 18 doctor practice offers an onsite membership fitness center and a gourmet breakfast and lunch bar. A wide atrium leads to broad multistory windows looking toward the Rocky Mountains and a meditation garden. It houses state-of-the-art technology, a spa and a yoga study. A truly exceptional aspect to Dr. Collins's practice is his role as "The Cooking Cardiologist®." Dr. Collins now conducts weekly cooking exhibitions in the full demonstration kitchen within the practice to help people learn to crave heart healthy foods.

ROB LEIGHTON, FOUNDER, KARDEA NUTRITION

Rob's passion for good food is as much a part of his genetic code as is high cholesterol. When Rob turned 47, blood tests indicated his cholesterol levels bordered on high. This fact was hardly surprising. His mother's cholesterol was high enough for her to participate in early clinical trials for cholesterol-lowering medications. Her mother had suffered multiple strokes, and her father died from a circulatory condition.

In a brief discussion, Rob's doctor told him to change his diet to lower his cholesterol, but no specific guidance about heart healthy foods to eat. He was told that if he was unable to achieve healthy cholesterol levels, he would be put on prescription cholesterol-lowering medications such as statin drugs.

"I was not philosophically opposed to taking medications to manage my cholesterol levels," Rob recalls, "but the prospect of taking cholesterol medication for decades was not attractive." It was more than just the length of therapy that bothered him. He also watched his parents, both in their 80s, spend a significant portion of their day organizing the cocktail of medications prescribed by an array of physicians. He was simply not ready to start down this road.

For Rob, many of life's magic moments occur over a meal. He has little interest in shopping for clothes or gadgets, but will happily wander the aisles of gourmet food stores, farmers' markets and ethnic delicatessens. While some may end the day with a novel, Rob is more likely to read good cookbook.

Rob also comes from the food industry. He spent 15 years as a senior executive with a chocolate manufacturer. In founding Kardea Nutrition, Rob combines his love and knowledge of food with a desire to use the best natural solutions to support heart health.

SUSAN BUCKLEY, CONSULTING REGISTERED DIETITIAN

A registered dietitian and nutrition educator, works daily with clients seeking to change their eating habits and eating ways. She integrates heart healthy nutrition and weight loss. Susan coaches based partly from personal experience. More than 15 years ago, she found herself 70 pounds overweight. Step-by-step, she shed those pounds in a year and she has kept off the weight.

With her patients, Susan works on two levels. The first is the rational side of moving to healthier eating. It is about education, making sure people understand what they should eat and what they should not eat. She helps them think about how to eat better and how many calories can be eaten to achieve a target weight over a reasonable length of time.

On another level, Susan works with her patients to understand why they eat. In many cases, patients find that the unhealthy calories consumed have nothing to do with being hungry. Rather, eating is used to cope with stress, anxiety and sadness as well as boredom. Discovering what drives their eating helps her patients move toward making healthier choices.

Join us in the
Kardea Kitchen

Are you interested in more heart healthy recipes and cooking techniques? Do you want recommendations about restaurants serving heart healthy meals? Looking to stay informed about the latest studies on nutrition and cardiovascular health?

Continue your journey to smart and delicious eating in the Kardea Kitchen at

www.kardeakitchen.com